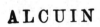

ALCUIN

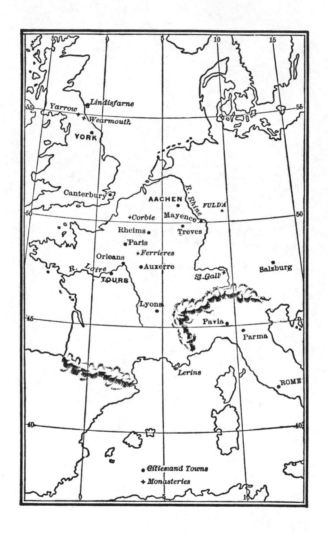

𝕿𝖍𝖊 𝕲𝖗𝖊𝖆𝖙 𝕰𝖉𝖚𝖈𝖆𝖙𝖔𝖗𝖘

EDITED BY NICHOLAS MURRAY BUTLER

ALCUIN

AND

THE RISE OF THE CHRISTIAN
SCHOOLS

BY

ANDREW FLEMING WEST

PROFESSOR IN PRINCETON COLLEGE

GREENWOOD PRESS, PUBLISHERS
NEW YORK

LB
125
A4
W4
1969a

Originally published in 1892
by Charles Scribner's Sons

First Greenwood Reprinting 1969

Library of Congress Catalogue Card Number 69-14147

SBN 8371-1635-X

PRINTED IN UNITED STATES OF AMERICA

PREFACE

It is the purpose of this book to present a sketch of Alcuin in his relations to education, with prefatory and supplementary matter sufficient to indicate his antecedents and also his connections with later times. The account given is based mainly on a study of Alcuin's writings, and attempts, so far as possible, to let Alcuin speak for himself, rather than to theorize about him. Such books about Alcuin and his pupils as have been found serviceable have also been freely consulted. In submission to the present custom of historical writers, and the authority of Shakspeare, I use the name Charles the Great in place of Charlemagne.

ANDREW F. WEST.

Princeton College,
September, 1892.

▼

CONTENTS

ALCUIN

AND

THE RISE OF THE CHRISTIAN SCHOOLS

INTRODUCTORY

At the mid-point between ancient and modern history stands the commanding figure of Charles the Great. The centuries of the Middle Ages which precede him record the decadence and final extinction of ancient institutions, while the nearly equal number of centuries which follow up to the time of the Renaissance and Reformation record the preparation for modern history. Thus, as finisher of the old order of things and beginner of the new, he is the central secular personage in that vast stretch of time between antiquity and the modern world, which we call the Middle Ages.

The fortunes of education during these fifteen centuries fall in well with the character of the periods which mark the successive phases of civilization in the West. Before Charles there are two periods, the one extending through the first four centuries of the Christian era and characterized by the decline of the imperial Roman schools of learn-

1

ing and the concurrent rise of Christianity; and the
other embracing nearly four centuries more, a time
of confusion, of barbarian inroads, of the dying out
of schools, and of prevalent intellectual darkness.
Then begins, under Charles at the end of the eighth
century, a third period, marked at its outset by the
first general establishment of education in the Middle Ages, an establishment lasting, however, but a
generation or two, and falling into ruin as a new
barbarism overran Europe. This period lasted well
into the eleventh century, when a fourth and last
medieval period began with a second restoration
of learning under the influence of scholasticism,
founding the universities, but itself finally decay-
ing and coming to an end at the Renaissance, that
third and final revival of learning which was so
radical and powerful as to become the beginning
of our modern age in education.

These are the three revivals of learning in the
West, each in turn stronger than its predecessor.
But the first one under Charles and Alcuin, though
the weakest, is yet of vital importance as a first
stage in the evolution of modern education. Narrow and technical as was the instruction given,
and brief as was the duration of the institutions
founded, it still remains true that Charles was the
first monarch in the history of Europe, if not of the
world, to attempt an establishment of universal
gratuitous primary education as well as of higher
schools. Moreover, as the result of Alcuin's organ-
izing sagacity, a body of men devoted to teaching

as well as learning was created, giving some degree of continuity to education down to the founding of the universities and so sheltering studies in various monasteries and cathedrals that some of the greater schools thus kept alive, or offshoots from them, afterwards became natural receptacles for the new university life of the next age.

CHAPTER I

THE SEVEN LIBERAL ARTS

THE seven liberal arts which embraced the studies constituting the curriculum of school education in the Middle Ages were an inheritance from classical antiquity. Their origin is to be sought in Greek education. Thus Aristotle in his *Politics*[1] defines "the liberal sciences" (ἐλευθέριοι ἐπιστῆμαι) as the proper subjects of instruction for free men who aspire not after what is immediately practical or useful, but after intellectual and moral excellence in general, and mentions several of these studies separately. By his time the educational doctrine of the Greeks had become highly developed and exhibited the ideals towards which the best Greek minds endeavored to direct their educational practice. We are not to suppose that by the terms "liberal arts," "liberal studies" and "liberal sciences" they meant either the whole of human knowledge or even the whole of liberal culture, for although the terms are not always employed in a uniform sense, yet they have a proper sense which must be held clearly in mind, if we would avoid confusion. Their proper meaning is this, — the circle of disciplinary school

---

[1] VIII, 1. For a full notice of the liberal arts in Greek writers see the Appendix to Davidson's *Aristotle* in this series.

4

studies which minister to the general education of youth, preparatory to the higher liberal studies, which are compendiously called philosophy. The distinction between the liberal arts and philosophy thus contains in germ the distinction between what we now mean by gymnasial and university education. It is of course true that the liberal arts were not always spoken of consistently, and that the practice of Greek writers may be compared in general with the varying modern use of the word "education," but it is no less true that to the Greeks the liberal arts primarily meant the circle of school studies. In fact they are often identical with school education itself, so that the saying of Pythagoras, "Education must come before philosophy,"[1] meant to the Greeks that training in the liberal arts must precede the higher culture. Philosophy also, as the goal of the earlier studies, is not infrequently styled a liberal art, sometimes the only truly liberal art. Thus Aristotle affirms, "It alone of the sciences is liberal, because it exists solely for its own sake and is not to be pursued for any extraneous advantage."[2]

The studies which came to be regarded as liberal arts were grammar, rhetoric, dialectics, music, arithmetic, geometry, and astronomy. It is not clearly known when each of these began to be considered as a school study, or how many of them were commonly so pursued, or that they were the only

[1] Πρὸ φιλοσοφίας παιδεία, Stobæus, *Serm.* XLI.
[2] *Metaphysics*, I, 2.

liberal arts. The Greeks did not formulate an unalterably fixed body of studies, seven in number. No list of seven arts nor any mention of seven as the number of the liberal arts is to be found in the Greek writers. However, there was an order in which they were pursued, and the first three, grammar, rhetoric, and dialectics, were preparatory studies which were generally pursued in the order stated. The other four disciplines usually came later, and it is probable that only a portion of those who had completed their grammar, rhetoric, and dialectics passed on to the music, arithmetic, geometry, and astronomy, and that only a portion of those who so passed onward studied all the four latter arts. It is clear, however, that the Greeks came to consider acquaintance with the liberal arts as a general education, and the only general education.

By the time of Cicero (B.C. 106–43) the *artes liberales* had passed over to Rome and become the groundwork of the education of the Roman *liber homo*, or gentleman. Cicero's references to the arts are abundant and instructive, furnishing as they do ample evidence of the familiarity of educated Romans of the late Republic with the studies of the Greeks. But it was not the writings of Cicero that saved the liberal arts for the Middle Ages. For this we must look to the monumental work, now lost, of his learned contemporary Varro (B.C. 116–27). It is fortunate indeed that such a writer, in his *Libri Novem Disciplinarum*, gave a

THE SEVEN LIBERAL ARTS 7

full account of the arts which had passed over from
Greek into Roman education. His list of "disciplines," as worked out by Ritschl,[1] is the following:
grammar, dialectics, rhetoric, geometry, arithmetic,
astrology, music, medicine, architecture. Astrology of course answers to astronomy, and the first
seven studies in his list are consequently the well-

[1] *Opuscula*, III, 371.
Boissier in his *Etude sur la Vie et les Ouvrages de M. T.
Varron* argues against the certainty of Ritschl's identification
of the "nine disciplines," holding that only six are clearly made
out.

In his treatise on the *Libri Novem Disciplinarum* of Varro,
now published in the third volume of his *Opuscula*, Ritschl
gathered and co-ordinated with marvelous acuteness the many
scattered fragments and ancient notices connected with Varro's
work, and concluded that he had identified each one of the "nine
disciplines" with reasonable certainty and their order of presentation in Varro with a fair degree of probability. Boissier says
Ritschl afterwards doubted whether he had sustained his identification of all the nine with sufficient proof. I have been unable
to find the passage where Ritschl avows such a change of con-
viction.

Fortunately, it is not necessary to re-examine Ritschl's elaborate array of evidence in order to find out what Varro's "nine
disciplines" were, since there is at hand a simple piece of proof
which covers the whole case. The account of the arts in Martianus Capella's *De Nuptiis Philologiæ et Mercuriæ* is demon-
strably a popularized account of the studies described in Varro's
Libri Novem Disciplinarum. Varro's work dealt with nine
studies, one for each of his nine books. Martianus likewise
has but nine studies, and these are precisely the nine worked
out by Ritschl as Varro's "nine disciplines."

But even if only six on Ritschl's list were proved to belong to
Varro's nine, yet, since these six are likewise six of the nine of
Martianus, the presumption that the unidentified three of Varro
would match the remaining three of Martianus is very strong.

known arts of the Greeks, but medicine and architecture are added. It is very plain that Varro had
not in mind any limitation of the arts to seven,
and yet it would not be safe to assert he meant
that all his "nine disciplines" were liberal arts.
Perhaps he did, but more likely all he meant to
represent by the "nine disciplines" was the studies
generally, whether liberal or professional, which
the Romans had inherited from the Greeks.

Passing on to the time of the early Empire, we
may trace the course of the liberal arts in the writings of the younger Seneca (B.C. 8–A.D. 65) and
Quintilian (A.D. 35–96), both of whom were well
acquainted with the writings of Varro and refer to
him as their authority. In Seneca's famous *Epistle
to Lucilius* [1] on liberal studies, five of the arts are
enumerated and described in the following order:
grammar, and then music, geometry, arithmetic,
and astronomy. This, though incomplete, yet corresponds, so far as it goes, with Varro and the Greeks.
It is also true that he recognizes in his very next
letter [2] the distinction between rhetoric and dialectics; but it would be a mistake to suppose from this
that he recognized these seven as all the liberal arts,
or that he consciously recognized any unalterably
fixed list. Indeed he speaks in another letter [3] of
medicine as a liberal art, and may have followed

---

[1] *Epist. Moral.*, Lib. XIII, Ep. III, 3–15. Ed. Haase, Leipsic,
1886.

[2] *Epist. Moral.*, Lib. XIV, Ep. I, 17.

[3] *Epist. Moral.*, Lib. XV, Ep. III, 9.

Varro in doing so. Shortly after Seneca comes Quintilian, in whose writings the arts are more strictly co-ordinated as a complete course of school instruction. He speaks in his *Institutes of Oratory* of the departments of study which need to be pursued "in order that that circle of instruction, which the Greeks call ἐγκύκλιος παιδεία, may be completed."[1] He also mentions as such studies grammar, rhetoric, music, and geometry, making the geometry include arithmetic, geometry, and astronomy. These six might perhaps be regarded as really seven if we suppose that Quintilian combined dialectics with rhetoric, as was sometimes done; but in any event it is clear that he, like Seneca, had not formulated an exclusive list of seven or any other number. Yet it is also clear that as with the Greeks, so with the Romans, grammar remained the inevitable first study, with rhetoric and probably dialectics immediately following, and that the fourfold division into arithmetic, music, geometry, and astronomy held its own as a natural distribution for the succeeding studies.

The Roman civilization, and with it the education established in the imperial schools, passed on to its decline, partly from interior moral decay, partly by external barbarian assault, and even more irrevocably through the supplanting power of the new ideals introduced by Christianity. We are chiefly concerned with the last of these, and more particularly here with the twofold attitude

[1] *Institutio Oratoria*, I, cap. 10, 1. Ritschl, *Opuscula*, III, 354.

assumed by the early Church of the West towards the arts. The first position was one of antagonism. Thus Tertullian proscribes pagan learning as both ineffectual and immoral, — apparently a most harsh and indefensible judgment. But if we keep in view the utter vileness of a great number of the so-called professors or teachers of the arts in the time of the Empire, a fact easily proven from the writings of Seneca and Quintilian, and the gross immoralities of pagan religion which were a natural development of so much of the mythology that tainted their literature, it will be seen that an antagonistic attitude to certain phases of pagan culture was inevitable from the first on the part of the Church, and this might easily pass into a proscription of the liberal arts. "The patriarchs of philosophy," says Tertullian, "are the patriarchs of heresy." He also decries them as "hucksters of philosophy and rhetoric." Lactantius says, "They do not edify but destroy our lives," and even Augustine calls them "croaking frogs." "Refrain from all the writings of the heathen," is the language of the Apostolical Constitutions,[1] "for what hast thou to do with strange discourses, laws, or false prophets, which in truth turn aside from the faith those who are weak in understanding? For if thou wilt explore history, thou hast the Books of the Kings; or seekest thou for words of wisdom and eloquence, thou hast the Prophets, Job, and

[1] Quoted and translated in Mullinger's *Schools of Charles the Great*, p. 8.

the Book of Proverbs, wherein thou shalt find a more perfect knowledge of all eloquence and wisdom, for they are the voice of the Lord, the only wise God. Or dost thou long for tuneful strains, thou hast the Psalms; or to explore the origin of things, thou hast the Book of Genesis; or for customs and observances, thou hast the excellent law of the Lord God. Wherefore abstain scrupulously from all strange and devilish books." Such is an authoritative utterance of the early church, so that we need feel no surprise at finding it echoed by her great doctors. Was it not Augustine who made famous the saying, *Indocti cœlum rapiunt,* "It is the ignorant who take the kingdom of Heaven"; and did not Gregory the Great assert that he would blush to have Holy Scripture subjected to the rules of grammar?

But though antagonism was the first position of the Church, and a necessary position in her first encounter with paganism, there were influential voices raised on the other side, and this harsh opinion was gradually modified, so that by the fourth and fifth centuries it was superseded by a better view. The liberal arts and their sequel, the ancient philosophy, came to be regarded with qualified approval, and despite his other utterances which embody the earlier attitude of the Church, it was again the great Augustine (A.D. 354–430), the literary as well as the theological leader of Western Christendom in his time, who was most influential in committing the Church to

a recognition of the arts and philosophy as suitable
studies for the Christian. This was accomplished
on the ground that they were useful — nay, even
necessary, for the understanding of the Scriptures.
His views are best set forth in his treatise, *On
Christian Instruction*, which was completed in his
seventy-second year, and may therefore be assumed
to represent his final judgment. Nothing freer or
more comprehensive has been said even under the
light of later Christianity than the maxim he has
there recorded, *Quisquis bonus verusque Christianus
est, Domini sui esse intelligat, ubicumque invenerit
veritatem,* " Let every good and true Christian know
that truth is the truth of his Lord and Master, wheresoever it be found." [1]   Such words foreshadow the
whole revolution in the ideals of education introduced by Christianity. In the same treatise he draws
a beautiful though fanciful parallel between Israel
and the Egyptians at the time of the Exodus, and the
similar situation of the Christians of his time, emerging from the spiritual bondage of paganism.   " As
the land of Egypt," he writes, " contained idols for
Israel to abominate and grievous burdens for them
to flee, yet there were also vessels and ornaments
of gold and silver, which Israel going out of Egypt
took with them to devote to a better use, not of
their own right, but at the command of God, the
Egyptians themselves unwittingly furnishing what
they themselves had been putting to an evil use.
So all the teachings of the heathen contain vain

[1] *De Doctrina Christiana*, II, cap. 17.

and idolatrous inventions and grievous burdens ot
unnecessary labor, and every one of us as we go
out from heathendom, under Christ our Moses,
ought to abominate the one and flee the other.
Yet there are likewise the liberal disciplines, well
suited to the service of the truth, and containing,
moreover, very useful moral precepts and truths
regarding the worship of the one true God. This
is their gold and silver, which they have not
created themselves, but have extracted from certain
ores, as it were, of precious metal, wheresoever
they found them scattered by the hand of divine
providence. So, also, they have raiment, the human institutions and customs wherewith they are
clothed. These we need for our life here below,
and should appropriate and turn them to a better
use. For what else than this have many of the
good and faithful done? Behold how that most
persuasive doctor and blessed martyr Cyprian came
out of Egypt, laden with what great spoil of their
gold and silver and raiment! How much did not
Lactantius take! and Victorinus, and Optatus, and
Hilary, not to speak of those now living or of the
innumerable Greek fathers. Moses also, that most
faithful servant of God, did so long ago, for is it
not written that he was learned in all the wisdom
of the Egyptians?"[1] Spoil the Egyptians! Take
their gold and silver and raiment. Take all the
truths of the pagan schools and use them in the
service of Christ. Henceforth the Christian is

[1] *De Doctrina Christiana*, II, cap. 40.

not shut up to rejecting or taking secular culture as a whole, but he is to select the best. A middle course, which is not a mere compromise, is thus opened up, avoiding the extreme of Tertullian in proscribing secular learning and the other later extreme of the Renaissance in taking all, whether base or excellent.

Let us not be misled into supposing that Augustine thought the arts or philosophy were to be studied purely for their own sake. Not so, — for he reasons that if the spoil of Egypt taken by Israel was great, yet the treasures of Solomon in Jerusalem were far greater. Accordingly he writes: "As was the amount of gold and silver and raiment taken by Israel out of Egypt when compared with the treasures they amassed afterwards in Jerusalem, treasures at their greatest when Solomon was king, such is all knowledge, useful though it be, which is gathered from the books of the heathen, when compared with the knowledge of the divine Scriptures. For whatever man has spoken elsewhere, if it be harmful, it is here condemned; if it be useful, it is herein contained."[1] The Scriptures are the final test of the "harmful" and the "useful." They are even more, for they embrace whatever of human learning is useful. Inconsistent indeed is this position with Augustine's other statements and with his injunction to study the good things in the liberal arts, if it be true that these things are already in the Scriptures. It sounds like a

[1] *De Doctrina Christiana*, II, cap. 42.

late echo of Tertullian. But let it be remembered
that Augustine represents in himself the history
of the differing successive attitudes of the Church
towards pagan culture, and that the general tenor
of his writings is decidedly in favor of studying
the arts and philosophy, though not solely or
principally for themselves, but as ancillary to the
supreme spiritual teachings of the Bible.

Augustine's connections with the liberal arts are
even more definite. He had himself been a teacher
of rhetoric before his conversion, and a writer on
seven of the arts. The record of this, in his
Retractations, which was written shortly before
427, is of distinct importance, particularly from
the fact that he was well acquainted with the writings of Varro, to whom he frequently refers as his
greatest authority. He states that while at Milan
awaiting baptism, he endeavored to write *Disciplinarum Libri* (almost the title of Varro's old work),
and that he finished only a book on grammar and
part of another on music.[1] After his baptism he returned to Africa and continued what he had begun
at Milan. Besides the two treatises mentioned, he
says that he wrote *de aliis vero quinque disciplinis
similiter inchoatis*, that is, finished books he had
begun upon five other disciplines, in addition to
grammar and music. It has been held by many with
Ritschl[2] that this means "on the other five disciplines," and that Augustine consequently recognizes

[1] *Retractationes*, I, cap. 6.
[2] *Opuscula Philologica*, III, 354.

seven as the total number of the liberal arts. But such cannot be proved from this passage, because it is possible that *de aliis quinque disciplinis* means "on five other disciplines." It is clear, however, that Augustine enumerates seven arts which he recognizes as liberal, and that he nowhere else recognizes more.[1] His list is as follows: Grammar and music, as above stated, and besides them the following "five other disciplines": dialectics, rhetoric, geometry, arithmetic, and philosophy. Elsewhere[2] he speaks of pursuing *memoratum disciplinarum ordinem*, a previously cited "order of the disciplines," and in still another passage[3] of having studied in his youth *omnes libros artium quas liberales vocant*, "all the books of the so-called liberal arts." Taking all his statements in one view it becomes plain that Augustine listed only seven liberal arts, and that he refers to a fixed order among them and to his acquaintance with each one. His list is remarkable in one respect, for astronomy is lacking and in its place we find philosophy, a substitution apparently due to Augustine's deep abhorrence of astrol-

[1] Nor does he seem to recognize less than seven in any general account of the arts. It is true that in another work (*De Ordine*, lib. II), when giving a general description though not making out a formal list, he names only six, — grammar, rhetoric, dialectics, music, geometry, astronomy. But he describes seven, for he treats of arithmetic, or "numbers," under the geometry. Thus in this account he deals with the same disciplines as in the *Retractations*, except that his favorite philosophy is replaced by the traditional astronomy.

[2] *De Ordine*, II, 16.   [3] *Confessiones*, IV, cap. 16, 30.

ogy as an impious art and his love for philosophy, which he puts in its place as the last and presumably the highest study.

But why should Augustine have only seven arts in his list? Certainly not by accident. He exercised some choice in the matter, as appears from his substituting philosophy for astronomy. Varro had written on nine disciplines, and though Augustine refers to him repeatedly as an authority, he does not adhere to Varro's number. The point is obscure. It may be Augustine knew of the seven arts in Martianus Capella's book, or that, though the arts were settling down to a body of seven by his time,[1] the limitation to seven was not definitely before his mind. The important point, however, in connection with Augustine, is not the number of the arts.

His position and influence may now be summarized with clearness. His settled view, attained after long meditation, was one of favorable regard toward the arts, principally because they ministered to the better understanding of distinctively Christian truths. Expressions of a different tenor are indeed to be found here and there in his writings. At one time he seems to go back to the idea that secular studies are useless, though not to be proscribed, and at another to advance fearlessly to the position that all truth everywhere is to be reverenced, in or out of the Scriptures, thus mirroring in his own

[1] Possibly through an Alexandrian influence, which we are unable to trace at present.

experience the early rigid attitude of the Church at the one extreme as well as the enlightened attitude of the distant future Reformation at the other, but finally resting midway between them. His influence was so commanding that from his time onward the Church was decisively committed to the toleration and even the encouragement of secular studies.

And yet Augustine does not stand alone in accrediting the liberal arts to the Christian Middle Ages. Another influence, potent, though at first reluctantly acknowledged by Christian writers, came from Martianus Capella of Carthage, who was either contemporary with Augustine or else somewhat earlier.[1] He wrote an allegorical treatise entitled *The Marriage of Philology and Mercury*, in a turgid, fantastical manner which had been fastened on the Latinity of North Africa by Apuleius. The book is consequently not only tiresome in its rhetorical luxuriance, but is often so involved and obscure that we are puzzled to determine whether the author's peculiarities in any given instance are due to his affected style or to an intention to be enigmatic. The object of the treatise, however, is quite

[1] The date of Martianus Capella was commonly supposed to be either in the 5th or 6th century of our era, until the appearance of Eyssenhardt's edition in 1866. He proves that Martianus Capella's book must have been written before the destruction of Carthage by the Vandals in 439, but is unable to show how long before. Parker argues that the book was written before Byzantium was called Constantinople, that is, before the year 330 (*English Historical Review*, July, 1890, pp. 444–446).

clear. It was to describe in a fanciful way the liberal disciplines of Varro. Martianus himself appears to have been a self-taught man. He set before him the writing of his book as a task for winter nights, and adopted the medley of prose and verse which had gained a place in literature through the influence of Varro's medleys, constructed in this fashion and known as *Saturæ*, as a proper literary receptacle for his rambling but copious account of the liberal arts. So he tells us figuratively at the end of his book that he has exhibited his literary goddess *Satura*, "prattling away as she heaps things learned and unlearned together, mingling things sacred with things profane, huddling together both the muses and the gods, and representing the cyclic disciplines babbling unlearnedly in an unpolished tale."[1] The "cyclic disciplines" are the liberal arts, the *encyclius disciplina* (ἐγκύκλιος παιδεία) of classical antiquity, and they become interlocutors in his allegory. The subject of his treatise, consisting of nine books, is the marriage of Mercury with Philology, the daughter of Wisdom. Mercury, as the inventor of letters, symbolizes the arts of Greece of heaven-born origin, while his bride, Philology, is an earth-born maiden representing school learning. After the consent of Jupiter has been given to this union of god and mortal,

[1] Loquax docta indoctis adgerans
Fandis tacenda farcinat, immiscuit
Musas deosque, disciplinas cyclicas
Garrire agresti cruda finxit plasmate.
— Book ix (closing lines).

the nuptials are celebrated in the shining **Milky Way** with the liberal arts as the seven bridesmaids. The first two books are occupied with the wedding and the other seven treat, each in turn, of the seven liberal arts in the persons of the bridesmaids. Grammar thus occupies the third book, dialectics the fourth, rhetoric the fifth, geometry the sixth, arithmetic the seventh, astronomy the eighth and music the ninth. The list is significant, for it tallies with that of Augustine, except so far as concerns astronomy, — a discrepancy of no importance, — and it differs from Varro in expressly omitting medicine and architecture, which had completed his "nine disciplines." As there is no evidence of any connection between the writings of Augustine and Martianus Capella, and good reason to believe that Augustine would not regard his purely pagan account with respect, especially as it contained contemptuous, though concealed flings at Christian doctrines, their agreement in keeping to seven liberal arts is remarkable and goes far toward proving that the arts were commonly supposed to be seven by or before the time of Augustine. Oddly enough, Martianus Capella never thinks of attaching any importance to the fact that they were seven, though he enlarges on the mystical character of the *Heptas* or septenary number [1] in other connections. Yet his limitation is none the less intentional, for medicine and architecture, which were very probably, if not certainly, two of Varro's nine, are expressly rejected

[1] pp. 262 and 265, Eyssenhardt's edition, 1866.

as bridesmaids. After six of the bridesmaids have
appeared before Jupiter and discoursed at length,
the Father of the Gods turns and asks Apollo how
many more of these excellent maidens are yet in
waiting. Apollo tells him that both medicine and
architecture are at hand, but adds, "Inasmuch as
they are concerned with perishable earthly things,
and have nothing in common with what is ethereal
and divine, it will be quite fitting that they be
rejected with disdain." Accordingly they are refused entrance, and music, the seventh bridesmaid
and "only remaining" heaven-born art, is given
audience.[1]

The meaning is plain. Medicine and architecture are excluded because they are not purely liberal studies. They do not elevate the mind to the
contemplation of abstract truth, but are of the
earth, earthly, and consequently unfit for the company of the celestials. They are of the useful and
professional arts. This limitation of the arts by
Martianus is therefore based on their character as
liberal studies, though the limitation to seven was
not due to reverence for that number. His arts

[1] "Superum pater . . . qui probandarum (=artium) numerus
superesset . . . exquirit. Cui Delius Medicinam suggerit Archi-
tectonicamque in præparatis adsistere, 'sed quoniam his mor-
talium rerum cura terrenorumque sollertia est nec cum æthere
quicquam habent superisque confine, non incongrue, si fastidio
respuuntur'" (p. 332). After further talk Jupiter answers,
"Nunc igitur præcellentissimam feminarum Harmonicam
(= Musicam) *quæ Mercurialium sola superest* audiamus" (p. 336,
Eyssenhardt's edition).

in the eyes of Christian writers were unbaptized
pagans, but the fact that they were seven did
much towards securing them a Christian standing.

After Martianus Capella, whose book was very
slow in getting in with the company of Christian
writings and consequently of exercising its strong
influence which came much later, the next name
of importance in the fortunes of the liberal arts is
that of the philosopher Boethius (481–525). His
is the last name in the history of ancient philosophy, and apart from a few expressions and terms
which bear a Christian aspect, he must be accounted
a pagan in his culture. His importance for the history of education is due to his translations of Greek
works which became text-books to a large degree
for the whole of the Middle Ages. He composed
versions or adaptations of treatises on arithmetic,
geometry, the logic of Aristotle, besides other writings of Aristotle and of Porphyry, and several
commentaries of his own, principally on Aristotle
and Cicero. This slender equipment was a chief
part of what was saved to the early schools of the
Middle Ages from Greek antiquity. Boethius has
left no general account of the seven arts, nor is
there to be found in his writings any indication
that he thought the number noteworthy in this
connection. His significance lies in the fact that
his writings served as text-books and as a source
for other writers on the arts to draw from. It
is perhaps worth noticing, however, that he is apparently the first to employ the term *quadrivium*

as the name for the combined study of music, arithmetic, geometry, and astronomy. It is also possible that the word *trivium*, as a formal designation for grammar, rhetoric, and dialectics, goes back to his time. At any rate, the substantial distinction between the *trivium* as an elementary course of study in language and discourse as opposed to the *quadrivium*, the later study of the sciences, emerges in his writings.

A contemporary and friend of Boethius, and like him, of noble family, was the Roman senator Cassiodorus (468–569), who retired in his old age from the turmoil of public life and the increasing barbarism of Italy under its Gothic rulers, taking shelter in his monastery in Calabria, where he spent his remaining years in the service of Christian learning. He attempted to stimulate the monks to unflagging study, particularly to the copying of manuscripts, and was in this way influential in extending the practice into most of the monastic orders of Latin Christendom. Besides rendering this important service to learning, he wrote assiduously both on Christian and secular subjects. One of his books is entitled *On the Arts and Disciplines of Liberal Letters*. He had previously written his book *On the Institutes of Sacred Letters* in thirty-three chapters, one chapter for each year of our Lord's earthly life. He thinks it fit, therefore, that his book on the liberal arts should also be divided into parts according to a suitable number. Seven is, of course, the one number that will match. Accordingly he opens his preface by saying : " It is now time that we should hasten through the text of the book we have in hand under seven other titles suitable to secular letters. Let us understand plainly that whensoever the Holy Scriptures mean to set forth anything as entire and complete, as they frequently do, it is comprehended under that number, even as David says, 'Seven times in the day have I spoken praises unto thee,' and Solomon, 'Wisdom hath builded her house, she hath hewn out her seven pillars.' " [1] Here is a new reinforcement coming from Scripture itself. The old plea of Augustine on their behalf was that the arts helped towards understanding the Scriptures, and although the fact that they were seven might naturally give them favor in his eyes, yet he had not thought to build an argument thereon. Cassiodorus uses this consideration as though it were a new one in connection with the arts, and however slight it may seem to us, it became forcible enough to the mystical-number worshippers of medieval times. The arts are seven and only seven. But this is the scriptural number for what is complete and per-

[1] " Nunc tempus est ut aliis septem titulis sæcularium litterarum præsentis libri (textum) percurrere debeamus. . . . Sciendum est plane quoniam frequenter quidquid continuum atque perpetuum Scriptura Sancta vult intelligi, sub isto numero comprehendit; sicut dicit David: 'Septies in die laudem dixi tibi ' . . . Et Salomon: 'Sapientia ædificavit sibi domum, excidit columnas septem' " (Migne, *Patrologia Latina*, LXX, 1150).

fect, and therefore the Christian must hold them in due honor.

His list of the arts is that found in Martianus Capella, to whom he is under evident obligations. But they are unacknowledged, and Martianus himself is only referred to in a contemptuous manner as a *Satura Doctor,* or undignified medley-writer. This much, however, may be assumed, that Cassiodorus adhered to the list of the arts he found in Martianus Capella, much as he must have abominated his undisguised paganism and pretentiously swollen style, and then proceeded to write a compend suitable for Christian use. His account is short and in no way original or forcible. The chapter on grammar is an abridgment of Donatus, the greatest of the Roman grammarians. His rhetoric is based to a considerable extent on Cicero. His dialectics come in part from Varro but principally from Boethius. It is really Boethius made easy for beginners. These three, grammar, rhetoric and dialectics, he calls arts, and the next four are called disciplines. Of his four disciplines, his arithmetic comes from Nicomachus and Boethius, his music from various sources, his geometry mainly from Varro and from the little of Euclid that was translated by Boethius, and lastly his astronomy from Boethius. Rudimentary and brief as his book is, it is not to be despised, for it was not so much the content as the spirit of his labor which had value. It helped to fasten the tradition of learning on the monastery and school life of centuries.

Thus far the liberal arts have been saved either
in treatises or compends, but the next writer who
gives them shelter accords them a small corner
in what was the first encyclopedia. This work is
the so-called *Etymologies* of Isidore, bishop of Seville in Spain (died 636). By his time barbarism
had wellnigh extinguished learning, and it is to his
labors that we owe the vast collection of excerpts,
gathered from patristic and classical writers, which
served as a thesaurus of all knowledge for centuries. Though his huge book is of course utterly
without original value and so full of absurdities
and puerilities that it may be considered as an
index of the retrogression in learning that had
set in, it is still true that Isidore was the most
widely informed man of his time. Braulio, bishop
of Saragossa, by whose persistent entreaty he was
induced to write the *Etymologies*, was next to him
the most learned man in Spain, and testifies that
Isidore was "distinguished in his knowledge of the
trivium[1] and perfectly acquainted with the *quadrivium*," and that God had raised him up in "these
last times" to save the world from utter "rusticity."
The liberal arts are briefly described in his book
and their proper number is expressly recognized
as seven: "*Disciplinæ liberalium artium septem
sunt.*"[2] His account of them is copied bodily from
Cassiodorus. A century and a half later Alcuin
admiringly regarded him as the *lumen Hispaniæ*

[1] The earliest instance I can find of *trivium* as a name for the
first three liberal arts.   [2] *Etymologiæ*, I, 2.

and as the one *cui nihil Hispania clarius habuit*,[1] expressions which reveal only too plainly how great must have been the darkness in which an Isidore could seem brilliant.

Such is the genealogy of the patriarchs of the liberal arts, and of these Boethius, Cassiodorus and Isidore became the acknowledged authorities in the schools, while Martianus Capella, though at first unacknowledged, was also influential. The learning they handed over did not attain to the dignity of a systematic exhibit of the learning of the ancients, but contained at best a general outline of its school studies imperfectly filled in and often faultily modified. It cannot be too plainly insisted on that what they gave to the Middle Ages was enclosed in a very few books and that this scanty store constituted practically the whole substance of instruction up to the eighth century, not being completely displaced until the Renaissance. Isidore stands last in the list, closing the development of Christian school learning in the midst of a barbarism that was extinguishing not only learning but civilized society in Western Europe. The darkness that followed his time for over a century was profound and almost universal. Rome itself had become barbarian, and only in distant Britain and Ireland was the lamp of learning kept lighted, not to shine again on the Continent until brought thither by the hand of Alcuin.

[1] *Alcuin*, Ep. 115, p. 477, Jaffé.

CHAPTER II

ALCUIN THE SCHOLAR AT YORK

A.D. 735-782

THE darkness on the Continent during the age following Isidore up to the time of Charles the Great coincides in time with the brightest intellectual eminence of the Anglo-Saxon Church, where learning found a shelter until it returned to Europe with Alcuin. Christianity had entered Britain by many doors and at many times, carrying with it the precious treasure of the liberal arts. From the great monastery at Lerins, off the Mediterranean shore of Gaul, St. Patrick had brought religion to Ireland, and other monks following him introduced not only the sacred but also the secular studies then flourishing in the Gallic schools. Both in the pagan schools of the dying Empire and in their Christian successors in southern Gaul the study of Greek lingered, and there was a directer and wider acquaintance with classical antiquity than elsewhere. Aristotle, Cicero, Virgil, Plautus, Varro, and Fronto were known and studied, and the dangerous Martianus Capella was the favorite handbook of the liberal arts. The quick and speculative Irish mind

28

was easily touched and responded to such teachings when brought into contact with them, and thus from the start developed in isolation from the stiffening and contracting influences which came to dominate the Latin Church on the Continent generally. This learning of Ireland passed in turn in the seventh century into Northumbria, the Anglo-Saxon kingdom of North Britain. To the south, Gregory the Great had sent the zealous monk Augustine in 596 to evangelize Britain from Canterbury as a centre. To the same place Theodore of Tarsus came in 669, soon to become its first archbishop. This strict and capable ecclesiastic succeeded in impressing on the Anglo-Saxon Church the Roman discipline and organization to a marked degree. But though a determined promoter of papal influence, he was yet a Greek by birth, and under his auspices the study of Greek was introduced in Canterbury. To the north the great twin monastery of Wearmouth and Yarrow had been founded and enriched with books from Lerins and other continental monasteries, and even from Rome itself. Benedict Biscop (628–690), its noble founder, also became its abbat. His greatest pupil was Bede (673–735), who at the age of seven began his education under Benedict and continued it under his successor, Coelfrith. He there "enjoyed advantages which could not perhaps have been found anywhere else in Europe at the time; perfect access to all the existing sources of learning in the West. Nowhere else could he acquire at once the Irish, the Roman, the Gallican, and the Canterbury learning; the accumulated stores of books which Benedict had bought at Rome and at Vienne; or the disciplinary instruction drawn from the monasteries on the Continent, as well as from the Irish missionaries."[1] All that he was capable of receiving from these several schools seems to have been grafted upon his simple and primitive Anglo-Saxon nature and made his own. His pursuit of learning was ardent and unremitting. Whatever of his time was not taken up in the round of monastic duties he devoted to his studies. "All my life," he writes, "I spent in that same monastery, giving my whole attention to meditating on the Scriptures, and in the intervals between the observances of regular discipline and the daily duty of singing in the church, I made it my delight either to be learning or teaching or writing." But Bede, though receptive, was conservative. Notwithstanding his allegorizing and inquiring habit of mind, he is yet above all marked by that loyalty and ancient simplicity of disposition which so strongly characterized the true Anglo-Saxon. He could therefore allegorize without being wildly erratic, as was Martianus Capella, so that he was in no danger from that source. More than this, his circumspect regard for the church tradition put such a pagan writer quite out of the reach of his acceptance. Consequently Bede never makes use of him, but follows after the feebler and safer Isidore, who was his

[1] *Dictionary of Christian Biography*, article on Bede by Bishop Stubbs.

favorite authority for all matters connected with the liberal arts. Even on his death-bed he dictated to a scribe some portions of Isidore's writings, giving as his reasons therefor, "I will not have my pupils read a falsehood or labor without profit after my death." One of his closest friends was Egbert, who became archbishop of York in 732 and founded there the cathedral school, enriching it with a great library. His rule of thirty-four years was of invaluable service to the cause of learning. Ælbert (Ethel bert), his *scholasticus* or master of the school, carried out his generous policy and afterwards succeeded him as archbishop. In this school they trained its greatest pupil, Alcuin.

Alcuin was descended from a noble Northumbrian family. The date and place of his birth are not definitely known, but it is very probable that he was born about 735 in or near York, where his early life was passed. While yet a little child he entered the cathedral school founded by Egbert, continuing there as a scholar and afterward as master until his departure for Frankland. In company with the other young nobles who composed the school he was first taught to read, write and memorize the Latin Psalms, then indoctrinated in the rudiments of grammar and other liberal arts, and afterwards in the knowledge of Holy Scripture. He has left on record in his poem *On the Saints of the Church at York* a characteristic description of the studies pursued under Ælbert. His verses read:

There the Euboric [1] scholars felt the rule
Of Master Ælbert, teaching in the school.
Their thirsty hearts to gladden well he knew
With doctrine's stream and learning's heavenly dew.

To some he made the grammar understood
And poured on others rhetoric's copious flood.
The rules of jurisprudence these rehearse,
While those recite in high Aonian verse,
Or play Castalia's flutes in cadence sweet
And mount Parnassus on swift lyric feet.

Anon the master turns their gaze on high
To view the travailing sun and moon, the sky
In order turning with its planets seven,
And starry hosts that keep the law of heaven.

The storms at sea, the earthquake's shock, the race
Of men and beasts and flying fowl they trace;
Or to the laws of numbers bend their mind
And search till Easter's annual day they find.

Then, last and best, he opened up to view
The depths of Holy Scripture, Old and New.

Was any youth in studies well approved,
Then him the master cherished, taught and loved;
And thus the double knowledge he conferred
Of liberal studies and the Holy Word.[2]

Under the fanciful coloring of this sketch, several
of the liberal arts may be discerned. Grammar
and rhetoric are there at the start. We may also
pick out two others, arithmetic, or "numbers," and
astronomy. "Jurisprudence" means canon law.

[1] Alcuin often calls York the *civitas Euborica*.
[2] *De Sanctis Eboracensis Ecclesiæ*, vv. 1430-1452.

The "storms" and "earthquakes," as well as the natural history of men and beasts, belong to Isidore's "geographical" information. This was commonly included under geometry, as pertaining to the description of the earth. "Aonian verse," "Castalia's flutes" and "Parnassus" are poetry in the sense of metrical exercises, and perhaps included some imitation of classical diction. Possibly music is also faintly hinted at in "Castalia's flutes." But though two of the liberal arts, music and geometry, are not clearly specified and dialectics is not named, we may be sure that Alcuin's picture is not intended to present a list but a freely drawn characterization of the studies at York, and it is fair to assume that the others were at least known, if not cultivated.

A lively gratitude for the learning he there received, but above all for the faithful instruction in Christian virtue which Egbert and Ælbert personally instilled, remained with him to the end of life. Long after he had gone to Frankland he wrote affectionately to the brethren of the school at York: "It is ye who cherished the frail years of my infancy with a mother's affection, endured with pious patience the wanton time of my boyhood, conducted me by the discipline of fatherly correction unto the perfect age of manhood and strengthened me with the instruction of sacred learning. What can I say more, except to implore that the goodness of the King eternal may reward your good deeds to me, his servant, with the glory of eternal blessedness?" Alcuin soon became the

most eminent pupil of the school and an assistant
master to Ælbert. On the death of Egbert in 766,
when Ælbert succeeded to the archbishopric, Alcuin
in turn appears to have succeeded him as master of
the school. At any rate, he was then ordained a
deacon, or "levite," and held the office of *scholasticus* for some time thereafter. Thus he might
naturally expect to succeed eventually to the archbishopric. On Ælbert's death in 780 he was given
charge of the cathedral library, then the most
famous in Britain and one of the most famous in
Christendom. He has left on record in one of his
poems a statement of the principal books which
were there stored, — a sort of metrical catalogue.
It runs in English as follows:

> There shalt thou find the volumes that contain
> All of the ancient fathers who remain ;
> There all the Latin writers make their home
> With those that glorious Greece transferred to Rome, —
> The Hebrews draw from their celestial stream,
> And Africa is bright with learning's beam.
>
> Here shines what Jerome, Ambrose, Hilary thought,
> Or Athanasius and Augustine wrought.
> Orosius, Leo, Gregory the Great,
> Near Basil and Fulgentius coruscate.
> Grave Cassiodorus and John Chrysostom
> Next Master Bede and learned Aldhelm come,
> While Victorinus and Boethius stand
> With Pliny and Pompeius close at hand.
>
> Wise Aristotle looks on Tully near.
> Sedulius and Juvencus next appear.

Then come Albinus,[1] Clement, Prosper too,
Paulinus and Arator. Next we view
Lactantius, Fortunatus. Ranged in line
Virgilius Maro, Statius, Lucan, shine.
Donatus, Priscian, Probus, Phocas, start
The roll of masters in grammatic art.
Eutychius, Servius, Pompey, each extend
The list. Comminian brings it to an end.

There shalt thou find, O reader, many more
Famed for their style, the masters of old lore,
Whose many volumes singly to rehearse
Were far too tedious for our present verse.[2]

The list of authors does not of course fulfil the
large expectations roused by Alcuin's glowing
promise of "all the Latin writers" in addition to
"those that glorious Greece transferred to Rome."
This spacious literary vista must be narrowed until
it includes only the comparatively few Latin and
fewer Greek writers, mainly ecclesiastical and only
in small part classical, which were available in
Alcuin's time. Yet single books meant something
then. They were objects to be treasured individu-
ally rather than shelved away by thousands. A
private collection of an hundred was so large as to
be thought remarkable. Hence it is easy to understand how the books in the York library, although

[1] For the sake of convenience in translation I have written
Albinus, the name of the learned abbat and friend of Bede,
instead of the absurd *Alcuinus* of some manuscripts or the
sensible, but metrically unmanageable *Alcīmus* of Froben's
emendation.

[2] *Versus de Sanctis Eboracensis Ecclesiæ*, vv. 1535-1561.

probably to be reckoned by hundreds rather than thousands, embraced substantially the whole of whatever learning there was.

Alcuin's list is therefore significant. Though the restraints of metre hindered him from including Isidore, yet with this exception the great school books of the time are mentioned, the books which were the basis of his activity as a teacher, first at York and afterwards in Frankland. Besides the unmentioned Isidore, whose writings were thoroughly familiar to him, he possesses Cassiodorus, Boethius and Bede, of the great medieval text-books. Of classical antiquity he has parts of Aristotle and Cicero, the poets Virgil, Statius and Lucan, and the grammarians Donatus and Priscian, as his chief authors. The fathers of the Latin Church were also in the library, and among them were books of Augustine, Jerome, Ambrose and Gregory the Great. The lesser authors who fill in his metrical catalogue exercise only a slight influence on his own writings. Whether any of the books in his list were in Greek is not a matter of much concern here. It is true that Theodore of Tarsus had brought in the teaching of Greek at Canterbury, his influence subsequently extending to York, and that the Irish influence was favorable to Greek studies, so that there were probably Greek books in the York library. But Alcuin, though he may have been acquainted with Greek sufficiently to read it a little, confined his own literary searchings to Latin. Accordingly, though Aristotle and some of the Greek fathers appear in his catalogue, it is more than likely that he is thinking only of Latin versions. All the Aristotle he employs may be found either in Boethius or in the treatise *On the Categories* falsely attributed to Augustine. His general school learning reposes conservatively on the old authorities, Boethius, Cassiodorus, Isidore and Bede. Even Boethius and Cassiodorus are more admired than used, so that he practically depends upon the other two. If Martianus Capella was in the York library, no mention of the fact is made.

Alcuin's fame as master of the school was great. He handed down to his pupils the learning he had received and imbued them with that desire of studying the liberal arts with which Egbert and Ælbert had indoctrinated him. He was well aware of the precarious condition of learning and impressed this fact faithfully upon his pupils. Years afterward, in a letter to Charles the Great, he recalled Egbert's fidelity in this respect. "My master Egbert," he wrote, "often used to say to me ' it was the wisest of men who discovered the arts, and it would be a great disgrace to allow them to perish in our day. But many are now so pusillanimous as not to care about knowing the reasons of the things the Creator has made.' Thou knowest well how agreeable a study is arithmetic, how necessary it is for understanding the Holy Scriptures, and how pleasant is the knowledge of the heavenly bodies and their courses, and yet there are few who care to know such things, and what is worse, those who seek to study them are considered blameworthy." Such was the spirit of his teaching and such the estimation in which he held up learning to the view of his pupils. Many flocked to hear him, and he soon became the best known master in Britain. And yet the names of only a few of his pupils at York have been handed down. One of them was Liudger, who came from the Continent to hear him, subsequently returning and becoming the first bishop of Münster in Saxony. If there were other foreign pupils, as is not improbable, their names are lost. The others, whose names remain, were Anglo-Saxons. Eminent among them was the younger Eanbald, who became archbishop of York in 796. He is the Symeon of Alcuin's letters. Three others stand next in prominence. They are Witzo, Fridugis, and Sigulf, who were so attached to their master that they followed him from York to Frankland. Witzo returned to Britain in 796, but the other two never came back. Another was Osulf, apparently the "prodigal son" over whom Alcuin grieved so deeply in his letters. He seems to be known later under the pseudonym Cuculus. Of his other pupils we know little beyond the names of Onias, Calwinus, Raganhard, Waldramn, and Joseph.

The continuity of his residence at York was broken by successive journeys which prepared the way for his final removal to the Continent. His first journey was taken in company with Ælbert before 766 into Frankland, and perhaps included a visit to Rome. The second journey was somewhat later, but earlier than 780. It was probably on this later visit that Alcuin stopped at Pavia, where Charles the Great was tarrying on his way homeward from Italy. Alcuin there attended the public disputation between Lullus the Jew and Peter of Pisa, the king's instructor in grammar, and thus came under the monarch's notice. His third visit was the one which resulted in transferring him from York to Frankland. It occurred early in 781, a few months after the death of Ælbert, whom the elder Eanbald succeeded as archbishop of York. Alcuin was sent by Eanbald to Rome to obtain from the Pope the archbishop's pallium. On this occasion he met Charles, who was again in Italy, at Parma, and was invited to leave Britain and make his home in Frankland, with a view to establishing learning in that kingdom. Alcuin hesitated, but promised to come in case he could obtain consent of his archbishop and of the king of his own country. He secured their consent and departed for the palace of Charles at Aachen in 782, thus finally giving up his place as master of the school at York.

CHAPTER III

ALCUIN THE MASTER OF THE PALACE SCHOOL

A.D. 782-796

ALCUIN arrived at the court of Charles, accompanied by a few of his faithful pupils from York, and entered at once upon his duties. Being at that time forty-seven years of age, his scholarship and character were already developed and seasoned. His impending task was not a further development of the learning he had received at York, but its introduction and diffusion in Frankland. For such a task he was admirably equipped, inasmuch as he brought with him all the prestige that came from being master of the best school of Western Christendom, and was additionally favored by the fact that the Anglo-Saxon scholarship he represented was of an eminently practical cast and therefore suitable for schooling the minds of the untutored Franks. He was also seven years older than Charles, a disparity in age sufficient to make him acceptable as the king's learned adviser and guide, and at the same time not great enough to interfere with sympathy and companionship.

The plight of learning in Frankland at this time was deplorable. Whatever traditions had found

their way from the early Gallic schools into the
education of the Franks had long since been scattered and obliterated in the wild disorders which
characterized the times of the Merovingian kings.
The monastic and cathedral schools that had for-
merly flourished were then rudely broken up, the
monasteries themselves being often bestowed as
residences on royal favorites and thus wholly
turned from a sacred to a barbarous use.   The
copying of books almost ceased, and all that can
be found that pretends to the name of literature
in this time is the dull chronicle or ignorantly
conceived legend.   There had indeed been a so-
called palace school, a centre of rudimentary
instruction for the court, but even in this studies
and letters played a very inconsiderable part as
one of the incidents of court life.   It was not
possible that learning should have at best more
than a precarious toleration, so long as the Franks
remained unsettled in their social order.   Exposed
on the south to their Saracenic foe, and on the north
and east to the stout Saxons and terrible Avars or
Huns, they were consequently in danger of being
ground to pieces between the two forces of Moham-
medanism and heathenism.   But in 732 Charles
Martel, the grandfather of Charles the Great, shat-
tered forever the Moslem hope of a conquest of
Frankland at the battle of Tours.   In 771 Charles
himself, on whom was to devolve the conquest of
the heathen Huns and Saxons, became sole king of
the Franks.   His earliest efforts, however, were

directed towards subduing the Lombards who had
given much annoyance to Pope Hadrian, —the first
step in that series of events which ended in establishing the spiritual supremacy of the papacy, on
the one hand, alongside of and supported by the
temporal supremacy of the emperor, on the other.
From 774 to 780 Charles was busy with the old
Moslem foe, still menacing his kingdom, though
unable to compass its destruction, and with the
more formidable Saxons. He visited Italy in 780,
when, as we have seen, he invited Alcuin to leave
Britain. In 781 he returned across the Alps to
his kingdom, and the next year received Alcuin
and installed him as master over the revived school
of the palace. The next eight years (782–790)
witnessed his continuous furtherance of Alcuin's
educational projects, first in the narrower circle
of the palace school and then in the advancement
of both higher studies and general rudimentary
education throughout his kingdom.

Let us enter the school of the palace at Aachen.
Alcuin sits as master assisted by the obedient three
who had followed him from York,—Witzo, Fridugis,
and Sigulf. Charles himself is foremost in eager-
ness among his pupils. Beside him is Liutgard,
the queen, the last and best beloved of his wives,
and not unworthy to be his companion in study.
Alcuin called her affectionately his "daughter,"
"*filia mea Liutgarda*,"[1] and his contemporary and
friend, Theodulf, the bishop of Orleans, celebrated

[1] Ep. 53, Jaffé.

in verse her nobility of character. His delineation is most lifelike and images the gentle queen at the court school, earnestly bending her mind to Alcuin's instruction. "Among them," he writes, "sits the fair lady Liutgard, resplendent in mind and pious in heart. Simple and noble alike confess her fair in her accomplishments and fairer yet in her virtues. Her hand is generous, her disposition gentle and her speech most sweet. She is a blessing to all and a harm to none. Ardently pursuing the best studies, she stores the liberal arts in the retentive repository of her mind." [1] Gisela, the only one of the four sisters of Charles of whom we have any full knowledge, was also a pupil, coming once and again to the school from her retirement as abbess of Chelles. The three princes, his sons, Charles, Pepin and Lewis, also attended, the last of these succeeding his father as emperor. Two of his daughters were also pupils, the fair-haired princess Rotrud and her gentler sister Gisela. There were also his son-in-law, Angilbert, and his cousins, the two brothers Adelhard and Wala, with their sister Gundrada. In addition to the members of the royal family there were Einhard, the king's intimate friend and later his biographer, Riculf, who became archbishop of Mayence, Alcuin's beloved friend Arno, who was later archbishop of Salzburg, and the able Theodulf, afterward bishop and archbishop of Orleans.

After the fashion of the time, Alcuin bestowed on

[1] *Carmina*, III, 1, Sirmond's edition, p. 184.

the members of this charmed circle fanciful pseu-
donyms and, as was his wont, justified the act by
Scripture. Explaining it in a letter to Gundrada,
whom he calls Eulalia, he writes, "Intimacy of
friendship often warrants a change of name, even
as the Lord himself changed Simon into Peter, and
called the sons of Zebedee the 'sons of Thunder,' a
practice approved not only in ancient times, but
in our modern day."[1] Alcuin himself assumed the
name of Flaccus, which he prefixed to Albinus, a
modified form of his own name. Charles is usually
called David, after the warrior king of Israel, and
sometimes is styled Solomon for his wisdom.[2]
Queen Liutgard becomes Ava, and his sister Gisela
is Lucia. His son Pepin is Julius, and of his two
daughters, Rotrud is Columba, and Gisela is Delia.
Angilbert is Homer, Adelhard is Antony, and
Wala is Arsenius. Einhard, his secretary, is Beze-
leel. Riculf is Damoetas. Arno, whose name
means an eagle, is appropriately called Aquila,
and Theodulf, the poetic bishop of Orleans, becomes
Pindar. Of his pupils from York, Sigulf is Vetu-
lus, Witzo is Candidus and Fridugis is Nathanael.
Another pupil, Rigbod, is called Macharius, and
Alcuin's fancy does not exhaust itself until he has
decorated Audulf, the seneschal of the palace, and
Magenfrid, the king's chamberlain, with the names

[1] Ep. 125, Migne.
[2] "Cernite Salomonem nostrum in diademate fulgentem sapi-
entiæ." *De Animæ Ratione*, in Migne, *Patrologia Latina*, vol.
CI, 649.

of Menalcas and Thyrsis, the two swains of Virgil.

It was no easy task that was set before him; for the court school was not only composed of untutored minds, but embraced among its pupils the youthful princes and princesses, and at the same time their elders, so that it is great proof of Alcuin's tact that he was able to interest and benefit such a heterogeneous circle. We may be sure that his instruction was largely conducted by the method of question and answer, Alcuin often preparing beforehand questions and answers alike, and that the substance of it at the start was grammar. And yet he went beyond this in his excursions over "the plains of arithmetical art," and in astronomy, rhetoric and dialectics, so that the palace school soon became the one centre within the royal dominions for the prosecution of higher studies.

The exigencies of his position demanded not only all his tact, but unflagging activity. He had to be more than a skilful teacher of docile pupils, for their awakened minds roved restlessly about from one question and puzzle to another, and with these they plied their master assiduously, not the least persistent of his questioners being the king himself. Charles wanted to know everything and to know it at once. His strong, uncurbed nature eagerly seized on learning, both as a delight for himself and a means of giving stability to his government, and so, while he knew he must be docile, he was at the same time imperious. Alcuin knew how

to meet him, and at need could be either patiently
jocular or grave and reproving. Thus, on one occasion when he had been informed of the great learning
of Augustine and Jerome, he impatiently demanded
of Alcuin, "Why can I not have twelve clerks such
as these?" Twelve Augustines and Jeromes! and to
be made arise at the king's bidding! Alcuin was
shocked. "What!" he discreetly rejoined, "the
Lord of heaven and earth had but two such, and
wouldst thou have twelve?" But his personal
affection for the king was most unselfish, and he
consequently took great delight in stimulating his
desire for learning. "O that I could forever
sport with thee in Pierian verse!" he writes, "or
scan the lofty constellations of the sky, or be studying the fair forms of numbers, or turn aside to the
stupendous sayings of the ancient fathers, or treat
of the sacred precepts of our eternal salvation."
Here is mention of several studies which they pursued together: poetry, — which we may here include
under grammar, — astronomy, arithmetic, the writings of the fathers, and theology proper, and of
these the king's favorite was astronomy. He
studied everything Alcuin set before him, but had
special anxiety to learn all about the moon that
was needed to calculate Easter. With such an eager
and impatient pupil as Charles, the other scholars
were soon inspired to beset Alcuin with endless
puzzling questions, and there are not wanting evidences that some of them were disposed to levity
and even carped at his teachings. But he was

indefatigable, rising with the sun to prepare for
teaching.   In one of his poetical exercises he says
of himself that "as soon as the ruddy charioteer of
the dawn suffuses the liquid deep with the new
light of day, the old man rubs the sleep of night
from his eyes and leaps at once from his couch,
running straightway into the fields of the ancients
to pluck their flowers of correct speech and scatter
them in sport before his boys." [1]   He begs Charles
to protect him against their levity, yet not because
he himself is weak, for he plainly says that the
old boxer Entellus is still equal to overthrowing
any youthful Dares. [2]

Books and studies were not his only care as a
teacher, for he was not wanting in plain speech in
regard to the lax morals of the court and of Charles
himself.   Whatever he gave in the way of private,
friendly admonition by word of mouth is of course
lost to us, but we have on record in his *Dialectics*
how he reasoned with the king on temperance as
one of the highest kingly virtues, and in the treatise dedicated to Gundrada (Eulalia) on *The Nature
of the Soul,* his pointed admonition, "Behold our
Solomon, resplendent with the diadem of wisdom.
Imitate his most noble traits.   Cherish his virtues, *but avoid his vices.*" [3]   When it is remembered that Alcuin's nature was peaceable, even to
timorousness, and that Charles was a man who

---

[1] *Carmina*, CCXXXI, Migne, CI, 782.
[2] *Carmina*, CCXXX, Migne, CI, 782.
[3] Migne, CI, 649.

could be fierce to cruelty, such faithful, plain
speaking on the part of Flaccus concerning his
King David seems no less heroic than was the
conduct of Nathan the prophet toward King David
in Jerusalem.   If, then, on occasion he did not
spare the monarch, whom he both loved and feared,
we are prepared to find the same faithful dealing
with his lesser pupils.   And such was the fact.
Again and again he exhorts both princes and princesses, by name, not only to be discreet and wise,
but to be chaste; and at least on the young prince
Lewis his teachings were not lost, for when he succeeded his father as emperor, though he fell short of
him in studies, he so far exceeded him in holiness
of life that he earned the title of Lewis the Pious.

The plans of Charles, however, were not restricted
to the palace school, important as it was as a centre and example for the learning he hoped to establish.   He did not intend to rule a barbarian kingdom.   Therefore he aimed to civilize and establish his people with Christian learning, and in this
of course Alcuin's counsel was indispensable and
his co-operation enthusiastic.   "If only there were
many who would follow the illustrious desire of
your intent," he wrote to Charles, "perchance
a new, nay, a more excellent Athens might be
founded in Frankland; for our Athens, being en-
nobled with the mastership of Christ the Lord,
would surpass all the wisdom of the studies of the
Academy.   That was instructed only in the Platonic
disciplines and had fame for its culture in the

seven arts, but ours being enriched beyond this with the sevenfold plenitude of the Holy Spirit, would excel all the dignity of secular learning." [1]

Acting under such impulses, Charles issued in 787 that famous capitulary, or proclamation, which is the first general charter of education for the middle ages. It is in the form of a letter to the abbats of the different monasteries, reproving their illiteracy and exhorting them "not only not to neglect the study of letters, but to apply themselves thereto with perseverance," and especially to choose out for this great work "men who are both able and willing to learn, and also desirous of instructing others." The capitulary is so important that it deserves complete presentation. It reads as follows in the only copy that has been preserved, the one addressed to Baugulf, abbat of the great monastery at Fulda:

"Charles, by the grace of God, King of the Franks and of the Lombards, and Patrician of the Romans, to Baugulf, abbat, and to his whole congregation and the faithful committed to his charge:

"Be it known to your devotion, pleasing to God, that in conjunction with our faithful we have judged it to be of utility that, in the bishoprics and monasteries committed by Christ's favor to our charge, care should be taken that there shall be not only a regular manner of life and one conformable to holy religion, but also the study of letters, each to teach and learn them according to his ability and the

[1] Ep. 86 Migne; 110 Jaffé.

divine assistance. For even as due observance of
the rule of the house tends to good morals, so zeal
on the part of the teacher and the taught imparts
order and grace to sentences; and those who seek
to please God by living aright should also not neglect to please him by right speaking. It is written 'by thine own words shalt thou be justified or
condemned'; and although right doing be prefer-
able to right speaking, yet must the knowledge of
what is right precede right action. Every one,
therefore, should strive to understand what it is
that he would fain accomplish; and this right
understanding will be the sooner gained according
as the utterances of the tongue are free from error.
And if false speaking is to be shunned by all men,
especially should it be shunned by those who have
elected to be the servants of the truth. During
past years we have often received letters from
different monasteries informing us that at their
sacred services the brethren offered up prayers on
our behalf; and we have observed that the thoughts
contained in these letters, though in themselves
most just, were expressed in uncouth language, and
while pious devotion dictated the sentiments, the
unlettered tongue was unable to express them
aright. Hence there has arisen in our minds the
fear lest, if the skill to write rightly were thus
lacking, so too would the power of rightly compre-
hending the Sacred Scriptures be far less than was
fitting, and we all know that though verbal errors
be dangerous, errors of the understanding are yet

more so.   We exhort you, therefore, not only not
to neglect the study of letters, but to apply your-
selves thereto with perseverance and with that
humility which is well pleasing to God; so that
you may be able to penetrate with greater ease and
certainty the mysteries of the Holy Scriptures.
For as these contain images, tropes, and similar
figures, it is impossible to doubt that the reader
will arrive far more readily at the spiritual sense
according as he is the better instructed in learning.
Let there, therefore, be chosen for this work men
who are both able and willing to learn, and also
desirous of instructing others; and let them apply
themselves to the work with a zeal equalling the
earnestness with which we recommend it to them.

"It is our wish that you may be what it behoves
the soldiers of the Church to be, — religious in
heart, learned in discourse, pure in act, eloquent
in speech; so that all who approach your house in
order to invoke the Divine Master or to behold the
excellence of the religious life, may be edified in
beholding you and instructed in hearing you discourse or chant, and may return home rendering
thanks to God most High.

"Fail not, as thou regardest our favor, to send a
copy of this letter to all thy suffragans and to all
the monasteries; and let no monk go beyond his
monastery to administer justice or to enter the
assemblies and the voting-places.   Adieu." [1]

[1] 1 Migne, *Patrologia Latina*, XCVIII, 895.   I have taken the
fine version of Mr. Mullinger in his *Schools of Charles the Great,*
pp. 97-99.

The voice is the voice of Charles, but the hand is the hand of Alcuin. The vigorous and commanding tone is the king's own, but he could never have devised the argument and cast it in the mould of the traditions of learning so perfectly unless he had been assisted by his master, and yet throughout the document the influences of Charles and Alcuin on each other are so happily blended that the mind and spirit that dominate it are one. It is not surprising, then, that it is the most important state paper of his reign on the subject of education; for although its application in practice was not lasting, and no enduring restoration of education was effected, yet this was neither the fault of the capitulary nor of the king. It was the necessary result of the insecurely protected social order. The bishops and abbats did respond in the lifetime of Charles and for a generation later; and while the society which he had ruled remained settled, so long the schools flourished, going down only in the general crash of the tenth century, when a new barbarism overran Western Europe. But though the schools founded under the stimulating influence of his exertions had but a short life, the capitulary itself remains to show us the great possibilities of the ideas which in inchoate form lay in his mind. First and most noteworthy is the assumption of the right of the state in the person of its sovereign, who is still only a king of the Franks and not yet head of the Holy Roman Empire, to compel a general attention to education, and in particular to see to it that the Church should keep up the study of letters. A second idea worthy of notice is that, without a due study and teaching of secular subjects, the servants of the Church will be unable to fulfil their proper functions and will be greatly hampered in understanding the Scriptures. The capitulary does not stop here, however, and insists both on the training of the monks and priests in learning, and moreover on the raising up of a body of teachers to perpetuate the great work of education, "men who are both able and willing to learn and also desirous of instructing others."

It is a pity that so few records of the time remain which cast light on the actual effect of the capitulary. Still there is no reason to doubt that it was generally obeyed, and there are not wanting evidences here and there of the institution of schools and of further commands of the king to extend and strengthen learning. In the very year in which the capitulary was issued, Charles, according to one of his annalists, "brought with him from Rome into Frankland masters in grammar and reckoning, and everywhere ordered the expansion of the study of letters; for before our lord King Charles, there had been no study of the liberal arts in Gaul."[1] We have also a letter from the king in 788 to the abbat of Fulda,[2] charging him to see to the schools in that place. In 789 a second capitulary was issued, laying down more definite instructions, and

1 Jaffé, *Monumenta Carolina*, p. 343, note.
2 *Epistolæ Carolinæ*, 3, Jaffé.

urgently enjoining their observance on the monks.[1] To this time, or perhaps earlier, belongs the so-called Homilary which Charles promulgated in order to promote the correction of the badly copied books of Scripture, containing the following significant passage: "As it is our desire to improve the condition of the Church, we make it our task to restore with the most watchful zeal the study of letters, a task almost forgotten through the neglect of our ancestors. We therefore enjoin on our subjects, so far as they may be able, to study the liberal arts, and we set them the example."[2]

Another capitulary, issued from Aachen in 789, gave further aid to education by insisting that candidates for the priesthood should be taken, not from the children of the servile class, but from the sons of freemen;[3] and, moreover, as late as the year 802, still another capitulary enjoined that "every one should send his son to study letters, and that the child should remain at school with all diligence until he should become well instructed in learning."[4] He secured promotion to influential sees of men who were learned and full of zeal in the cause of education. Such were Paulinus, the patriarch of Aquileia; Leidrad, the archbishop of Lyons; Arno, archbishop of Salzburg; Riculf, archbishop of Mayence; and Theodulf, bishop of Orleans. A report of Leidrad to Charles, concerning the schools established in his diocese, is still

[1] Pertz, *Leges*, I, 66.
[2] Pertz, *Leges*, I, 44.
[3] Baluze, I, 209.
[4] Pertz, *Leges*, I, 107.

preserved, from which it is clear that besides the
common village schools there was a cathedral school
maintained, and that it was in some sense preparatory to the school of the palace.[1] Theodulf, the
bishop of Orleans, carried out in his diocese the
instructions of his king most thoroughly by organ-
izing schools in every parish for the children of
all, enjoining upon the priests to exact no fees for
their teaching. His words are: "Let the priests
hold schools in the towns and villages, and if
any of the faithful wish to entrust their children
to them for the learning of letters, let them not
refuse to receive and teach such children. Moreover, let them teach them from pure affection,
remembering that it is written, 'the wise shall shine
as the splendor of the firmament,' and 'they that
instruct many in righteousness shall shine as the
stars forever and forever.' And let them exact
no price from the children for their teaching, nor
receive anything from them, save what their parents
may offer voluntarily and from affection." [2]

From these and other scattered notices, we are
able to form some notion of the extent to which

[1] *De Scholis celebrioribus seu a Carolo Magno seu post eundem
Carolum per Occidentem instauratis.* Launois, *Opera*, IV, p. 14.

[2] " Presbyteri per villas et vicos scholas habeant et si quilibet
fidelium suos parvulos ad discendas literas eis commendare vult,
eos suscipere ac docere non renuant, sed cum summa caritate
eos doceant. . . . Cum ergo eos docent, nihil ab eis pretii pro
hac re exigant, excepto quod eis parentes caritatis studio sua
voluntate obtulerint." Migne, *Patrologia Latina*, CV, pp. 191
and 207.

the ideas of the king were understood and also of the character of the schools established. Universal provision for elementary instruction was contemplated and to some extent carried out, and in Theodulf we see for the first time the assertion of the principle that elementary instruction should be gratuitous. Had it been possible to follow this up with the next and most natural step, namely, making of the elementary instruction not only universal and gratuitous but compulsory, the consequences would of course have been far reaching. But though Charles finally went so far as to enjoin that "every one should send his son to school to study letters and that the child should remain at school with all diligence until he should become well instructed in learning," the idea of organized compulsion does not seem to have crossed his mind. It was reserved for modern times.

In regard to the character of the schools themselves, it should be observed that they were not all of one sort. The palace school was unique. It was the chief centre of culture, a very rudimentary learned academy, but yet the head and centre of the education of the times. The other schools may be roughly divided into the monastic and cathedral in one class and the parish or village schools in the other. The monastic and cathedral schools gave elementary and, in some instances, superior instruction, while the village schools were purely elementary. The head of a village school was the parish priest. The head of a monastic school was

its abbat, who was responsible to the head of his
order and thus to Rome.   The head of a cathedral
school was the *scholasticus* appointed by the bishop
of the diocese, who in his turn was also answerable
to Rome.   But the abbats of the monasteries did
not acknowledge jurisdiction on the part of the
bishops over them, and this led to frequent conflicts
whenever the bishop attempted to exercise such
jurisdiction.   In fact, Alcuin himself was in this
way brought into unfriendly relations with his own
friend, Theodulf, the bishop of Orleans, at the time
when Alcuin was abbat of St. Martin in that diocese.   The monastic schools came to be divided
into two sides, the interior and the exterior school.
The interior school received only the *oblati*, that is,
boys who were offered for the monastic life.   The
exterior schools were attended by boys who were
not to be monks, but priests, and by those who were
intended for secular life.   In both the interior
and exterior schools instruction was gratuitous.
The episcopal or cathedral schools were neither so
strict nor so flourishing as the monastic schools,
whose exterior side they resembled, educating candidates for the priesthood and children of laymen
generally.   The scholars were partly maintained
by the endowments of the school and, in the case
of the laity, to some extent by the payment of
tuition.   Apart from the rigorous discipline of
monastic life exacted of the *oblati*, there is, however, no essential distinction to be drawn between the
instruction furnished in the monasteries and cathe·

drals. It began with learning to read and write,
the *computus*, or art of reckoning, the principal use
of which was to determine the church calendar, and
also the art of singing. Above this rudimentary
teaching came the study of grammar, to which great
pains was devoted, sometimes followed by rhetoric
and dialectics, with little or nothing beyond, except
in the greatest monasteries. Of course there was
also the study of Holy Scripture. In the village
schools nothing but the rudiments were taught,
except such scholastically unimportant additions as
the learning of the creed, the Lord's Prayer, and
perhaps parts of the Psalter.

Three stages or levels of advancement are thus
discernible in the education incompletely organized
by Charles and Alcuin. At the head of their
hierarchy of schools stands the palace school or,
to strain the expression severely, the university.
Underneath this and preparatory to it is the second-
ary teaching of certain monastery and cathedral
schools, while primary education is also found in
monasteries and cathedrals and is the exclusive
substance of instruction in the village schools.

In 790, after eight years of unsparing labor in
the conduct of the palace school and the furtherance of the king's wider educational projects, Alcuin
returned to York. Witzo, and then Fridugis, tem-
porarily took his place in the palace school. He
had never abjured his allegiance to the king of his
native Northumbria nor his obedience to the archbishop of York, regarding himself as only a so-

journer at the court of Charles.   It was therefore
natural, when the palace school had become well
established, and the king's commands for founding
other schools had been measurably carried out, that
Alcuin should regard his task among the Franks
as accomplished.   The limitations under which he
labored at the court must also have become plain;
for with all the lively interest in learning that was
awakened, there were no such stable guarantees
for its perpetuation visible in the disposition or
intelligence of the raw Franks as could be compared with the well-settled and vigorous tradition
of learning in Northumbria, — the only steady light
that had broken the general darkness for now
nearly a century.   The publicity of a court and the
journeying to and fro, whenever Charles moved
from Aachen, were far less congenial to him than
monastic seclusion, and where could he so naturally
turn for this as to his old home in York?   There
was the peaceful round of ecclesiastical life, there
was the great store of books, which he had sadly
missed at the court, there were his brethren and
some of his old pupils in the home of his youth,
and there accordingly was the true retreat for his
declining years.

A dissension had sprung up shortly before this
time between Charles and Offa, king of Mercia,
then the most powerful of the Anglo-Saxon rulers.
Charles, consenting to Alcuin's visit to Britain, gave
him letters to Offa and enabled him to act as an intermediary in effecting a reconciliation.   Arrived at

York, Alcuin found that Ethelred, in one of those
sudden mutations to which the affairs of the petty
kings of the Anglo-Saxons were so liable, had
become king of Northumbria. His cruelties and
excesses were shocking and went far to discourage
the hope of peaceful retirement with which Alcuin
had returned home. Successfully concluding his
peace-making negotiations with Offa, Alcuin found
himself not indisposed to obey the summons which
came from Charles to return to his court, where
there was new and urgent need for his services.
Accordingly he left York for Aachen in 792. Two
heresies had sprung up which threatened not only
the ecclesiastical unity of Latin Christendom, but
the peace of Frankland as well. One was the teaching of two Spanish bishops, Felix of Urgel and
Elipandus of Toledo, that Christ was not the Son of
God in the sense of being so by generation, except as
to his Godhead, while as to his manhood he was
not begotten but adopted. This effort to solve the
mystery attaching to the two natures in the person
of Christ was known as Adoptionism. Against this
heresy Alcuin vindicated the old Church doctrine by
several treatises, finally securing its condemnation
in 794 by the Council of Frankfort. It is a noteworthy fact that nowhere in his writings is there
any call upon the king to use his civil power to
crush the heresy. Nor does Charles seem to have
thought of doing so. It was well that he did not,
whether his forbearance was due to a sense of
justice, fondness for theological controversy, or

political expediency.   There is reason to believe
that all these motives were influential.   Had the
king resorted to civil punishment instead of re-
sorting to the more peaceful but equally potent
resource of ecclesiastical condemnation, the political danger was that the Spanish heretics, who were
numerous and obstinate, would join themselves to
his old Saracen foes in Spain and thus embolden
them to harass his kingdom.

The other heretical foe was also political in its alli-
ances.   Irene, the ruler of the Eastern Empire, had
done much to re-establish the worship of images,
and succeeded in carrying through her designs by
the aid of a dubiously constituted general council
held at Nice in 787.   At this council Pope Hadrian
was not recognized as in any way the head of the
Church, and consequently not only was the primacy
of Rome ignored, but the independence and unity
of the Western Church was thereby imperilled.
Hadrian's dilemma was painful.   He was not
ready to put the ban of the Church on image-worship in moderation, but felt bound to resist this
Eastern encroachment on his papal dignity.   If he
acquiesced in the validity of the council's restoration of image-worship, he thereby submitted to the
political tyranny of Irene and Constantinople.   If
he threw himself upon the sovereigns of the West
to support his independence, he must break with
the East and perhaps consent to condemn image-
worship, which the papacy had countenanced.
There was but one king able to aid him, and that

king was Charles.   So in 792, after long conceal-
ment and avoidance, Hadrian sent him the decrees
of Nice.   Charles of course could not endure that
the Pope should be in vassalage to his political
rival of the East, and was moreover an abominator
of image-worship.   Whatever languid eastern Christians might do, the independent Franks would never
prostrate themselves in abasement before the effigies
of saints.   He sent Alcuin the Nicene enactments,
urging him to refute them, and Alcuin devoted himself assiduously to his task.   It is in every way
probable that the so-called *Caroline Books*, which
appeared at this time as a work of Charles, refut-
ing the Nicene errors and exposing the idolatrous
character of image-worship, are really the work of
Alcuin.[1]   The Council of Frankfort, which Alcuin
attended by the king's request, not only dealt with
the Adoptionist heresy, but also proceeded to condemn the practice of image-worship and to reject
the authority of Nice, and as the result of this
council the two great theologico-political spectres
of the time of Charles were laid.

Meanwhile Alcuin's thoughts were being weaned
away from the idea of a return to his own land by
the incursions of the Norsemen on its coasts, and
especially by the horrible devastation of Lindis-
farne.   His longing for retirement grew stronger
and stronger and, after he had passed his sixtieth
year, became irrepressible.   He earnestly begged
Charles to let him go to Fulda and there end his

[1] *Monumenta Alcuiniana*, p. 220, note.

days in peace.   But Charles would not subject him to the rule of even the abbat of Fulda, and as the abbat of the venerable house of St. Martin at Tours died at that time (796), he appointed Alcuin in his stead.

CHAPTER IV

ALCUIN THE ABBAT OF TOURS

A.D. 796-804

THE monastery of St. Martin at Tours, on the banks of the Loire, was one of the oldest and richest in Frankland. Adjoining the church wherein the relics of St. Martin himself were enshrined, honored by gifts of the Frankish kings and hallowed by the devout visits of many a band of pilgrims, it was easily the first abbey within the dominions of Charles, not yet rivalled even by Fulda. Its rich endowments, consisting of landed estates scattered in various parts of the kingdom and tilled by thousands of serfs, yielded great revenues toward its support, so that when Charles appointed Alcuin to be its abbat, he conferred the highest monastic benefice within his gift, disregarding precedent in his zeal to do honor to his old teacher, who had no reason to expect such elevation, Alcuin not being a monk, but a simple deacon of the church at York. Yet he was a monk in spirit, "a true monk without the monk's vow," as his biographer admiringly writes, and Alcuin may have had such relations to monastic life at York as to make his selection at least ecclesiastically unobjectionable. The monks at Tours

64

had been living with less strictness than their vows required, and it was therefore Alcuin's first care to subject them to the rigorous rule of the Benedictine order. This was not accomplished without a strong effort, and the importation of brethren from other monasteries to assist in reviving the strictness he so desired to see practised. But Alcuin's efforts were not limited to a simple revival of the monastic life. His house was to be a centre not only of austerity, but of learning. His provident mind perceived clearly that if the learning which had been established with such pains in Northumbria was already in danger of destruction, and if, moreover, the learning he himself had brought thence into Frankland would lose a powerful protector after Charles should be gone, the best service which he could render by way of forestalling the uncertain outlook was to raise up by his own personal teaching, in the few years that remained to him, a body of pupils so devoted to learning and so considerable in number, that there might be good hope of passing on the tradition of studies through their hands. It was thus that learning had been saved before by being literally handed down from one teacher to the next, from Benedict Biscop to Bede, from Bede to Egbert, and from Egbert to Alcuin, so that in the eyes of such a respecter of traditional methods as Alcuin was, it might well seem the only way of discharging his duty in his turn.

Accordingly he set about his work with the same industry and zeal that had marked his earlier teach-

ing, though in a soberer and at times a severer
spirit. Soon after his installation at Tours, he
wrote to Charles a letter which furnishes glimpses
of the beginning of his work. "I, your Flaccus,"
he writes,[1] "following out your exhortation and
desire, strive to minister to some in the house of
St. Martin the honeys of Holy Scripture. Others
I seek to inebriate with the old wine of the ancient
disciplines, and still others will I begin to nourish
with the apples of grammatical subtlety. Again,
I endeavor to irradiate the minds of others with the
order of the stars, even as a painter would illuminate by his figures the dome of a church,[2] being
made all things to all men so that I may instruct
many for the advantage of the holy Church of God
and for the honor of your kingdom, that the grace
of Almighty God may not be found vain in me,
nor the generosity of your kindness of none effect."
There is something of the glow of his earlier years
in this allegorical description. He is once more at
his old work, teaching the Scriptures, teaching the
"ancient disciplines" or liberal arts, starting beginners in grammar, and instructing others more
advanced in the king's favorite study, astronomy.
The studies which he had begun to cultivate at
York, and introduced at the palace, he now trans-
plants finally to the abbey at Tours.

[1] Ep. 78 Jaffé; 43 Migne.
[2] The clause translated "even as a painter would illuminate
by his figures the dome of a church," is obscure in the text of
Alcuin's letter. I give what seems to be the meaning.

But his activity was straitened at first by the lack of books, and of this he informs the king, asking leave to send some of the younger monks to York to obtain them. "I, your servant," he continues, "lack the rarer books of scholastic erudition which I had in my own country through the devoted industry of my master Ælbert, and by my own labors. And so I mention this to your excellency, in the hope it may please the wisdom of your counsel that I should send some of the youth here to bring to us the necessary books, and thus fetch into Frankland the flowers of Britain, so that besides the 'garden inclosed' that is now in the Euboric city, there may likewise be in the Turonic city 'orchards of pomegranates with pleasant fruits,' and thus shall 'the south wind come and blow upon our gardens' along the river Loire 'that the spices thereof may flow out.' Thus indeed shall be fulfilled that which follows in the Book of Canticles,[1] whence I have taken this parable: 'My beloved shall come into his garden and eat his pleasant fruits,' and say to the youth: 'Eat, O friends! yea, drink and be drunken, O beloved!' Moreover the word of the prophet Isaiah exhorting to the study of wisdom shall also be fulfilled: 'Ho every one that thirsteth, come ye to the waters, and ye who have no money, come ye, buy and eat. Yea, come, buy wine and milk without money and without any price.'" What books Alcuin received from York as the result of this request we do not

[1] Solomon's Song iv, 12, 13, 16, and v, 1.

know, except that they were of course such books as he himself had access to when there. Isidore and Bede would naturally be sent for among the books on the liberal arts, and in fact we have knowledge of the copying of the works of Bede under Alcuin's supervision at Tours. There were undoubtedly many volumes of the fathers, which Alcuin felt necessary to have brought from Britain; for when he wrote elaborately some years before against the Adoptionist heresy and image-worship, he had to resort to the library at York to obtain his numerous quotations from the patristic writings. It is also worth noticing that the spirit in which he proposed to teach at Tours had the same liberality of intention which had characterized the capitulary of his friend and helper, Theodulf, enjoining upon the priests of his diocese to teach without exacting tuition fees. Such is the meaning of Alcuin's quotation from Isaiah: "Ye who have no money, come, buy and eat, yea, come, buy wine and milk without money and without any price." The thought of exacting pay for teaching was not in Alcuin's mind, and the fact that the teaching was gratuitous, while the value of what was taught was inestimable, seemed to him one of the strongest incentives to study on the part of his pupils. It is interesting to note, in this connection, some verses ascribed to him, and set up at a fork in the street of Salzburg where the way led in one direction to a tavern and in the other to a school. They read, "O traveler, hastening through the street! halt on thy way and

read these versicles studiously.   The one side will
lead him who desires drink to a tavern, but the
other is blest with a double advantage.   Then
choose, O traveler, which way thou wilt! either
to go and drink, or to go and learn from holy
books.   If thou wilt drink, thou must also pay
money, but if thou wilt learn, thou shalt have what
thou seekest for nothing." [1]

Let us return to his letter to Charles.   Nothing,
he says, is a loftier attainment or a pleasanter exercise, a stronger defence against vice, or more praise-
worthy in every way, than studies and learning, to
which we are exhorted in every page of Scripture.
Nothing, he reminds the king, is so excellent for
the young princes in the palace, now in the flower
of youth, as to pursue their studies, for it is these
which will bring them honor in their old age and
finally qualify them for eternal blessedness.   " According to the measure of my small ability," he
impressively continues, " I shall not be slothful in
sowing the seeds of wisdom among your servants in
these regions, being mindful of the saying: 'In the
morning sow thy seed and in the evening withhold
not thine hand, for thou knowest not whether shall
prosper, either this or that, or whether they both
shall be alike good.'   In the morning I sowed the
seed in Britain in the flourishing studies of youth,
and now, as my blood is growing chill at evening,
I cease not to sow the seed in Frankland, praying
that both alike may prosper by the grace of God."

[1] Migne, Vol. CI, 757, *Carm.* CXIX.

The evening is sensibly approaching, and Alcuin
grows more and more conscious of the shortness of
the time at his command. His purpose, however,
is only the more resolute, his desire the more earnest, that the good work he had begun in Britain and
continued in Frankland may prosper. And so he
sets himself busily to the consummation of his
work, and the abbey at Tours at once becomes the
best school in Frankland.

In addition to the strict enforcement of monastic
discipline and the instruction given in the school
both to candidates for the religious life and to the
laity, Alcuin was occupied in supervising the
copying of manuscripts in the *scriptorium*, and
the books that were made became models for
copyists thereafter. His careful particularity in
regard to punctuation and orthography, and his
employment of a clearer and neater form of letter,
are to be seen to-day as the distinguishing features
of the body of classical and patristic manuscripts
dating from the ninth century and written in what
are called the Caroline minuscules. Of course, the
books which issued from Tours are in no way to
be compared with the stately uncial manuscripts
of the late Roman Empire, but they are a vast
improvement, both in appearance and accuracy,
over the slovenly transcripts made in the time of
the Merovingian kings. Alcuin himself had served
as a copyist at York, and his treatise *On Orthography*
was in all probability the reference-book of the
scribes as they worked under his supervision at

Tours. There are not wanting indications in his writings of the scrupulous regard he paid to these matters, and of the discouraging ignorance on the part of scribes, which he had to overcome. In a letter written to Charles from Tours, in 799, he mentions the fact that he had copied out on some blank parchment, which the king had sent him, a short treatise on correct diction with illustrations and examples from Bede, and another containing "certain figures of arithmetical subtlety composed for amusement," and then adds apologetically: "Although the distinctions and sub-distinctions of punctuation give a fairer aspect to written sentences, yet from the rusticity of scribes their employment has almost disappeared. But even as the glory of all learning and the ornaments of wholesome erudition begin to be seen again, by reason of your noble exertions, so also it seems most fitting that the use of punctuation should also be resumed by scribes. Accordingly, although I accomplish but little, I contend daily with the rusticity of Tours. Let your authority so instruct the youths at the palace that they may be able to utter with perfect elegance whatsoever the clear eloquence of your thought may dictate, so that wheresoever the parchment bearing the royal name shall go, it may display the excellence of the royal learning." [1] A very delicate hint to Charles to mind his commas and colons, and to see that the princes at Aachen did the same, as well as a lament for the general disregard of the

[1] Ep. 101 Migne; 112 Jaffé.

accuracies and niceties of writing. Alcuin's injunctions to the scribes at Tours were repeated more than once and found expression in some of his verses which seem to have been affixed to the entrance of the *scriptorium* as a permanent warning. They run as follows:[1] " Here let the scribes sit who copy out the words of the Divine Law, and likewise the hallowed sayings of holy fathers. Let them beware of interspersing their own frivolities in the words they copy, nor let a trifler's hand make mistakes through haste. Let them earnestly seek out for themselves correctly written books to transcribe, that the flying pen may speed along the right path. Let them distinguish the proper sense by colons and commas, and set the points, each one in its due place, and let not him who reads the words to them either read falsely or pause suddenly. It is a noble work to write out holy books, nor shall the scribe fail of his due reward. Writing books is better than planting vines, for he who plants a vine serves his belly, but he who writes a book serves his soul."

We can almost reconstruct the scene. In the intervals between the hours of prayer and the observance of the round of cloister life, come hours for the copying of books under the presiding direction of Alcuin. The young monks file into the *scriptorium*, and one of them is given the precious parchment volume containing a work of Bede or Isidore or Augustine, or else some portion of the

[1] Migne, CI, 745, *Carm.* LXVII.

Latin Scriptures, or even a heathen author. He
reads slowly and clearly at a measured rate while
all the others seated at their desks take down his
words, and thus perhaps a score of copies are made
at once. Alcuin's observant eye watches each in
turn and his correcting hand points out the mistakes
in orthography and punctuation. The master of
Charles the Great, in that true humility that is the
charm of his whole behavior, makes himself the writ-
ing-master of his monks, stooping to the drudgery of
faithfully and gently correcting their many puerile
mistakes, and all for the love of studies and the
love of Christ. Under such guidance and deeply
impressed by the fact that in the copying of a few
books they were saving learning and knowledge
from perishing, and thereby offering a service most
acceptable to God, the copying in the *scriptorium*
went on in sobriety from day to day. Thus were
produced those improved copies of books which
mark the beginning of a new age in the conserving
and transmission of learning. Alcuin's anxiety in
this regard was not undue, for the few monasteries
where books could be accurately transcribed were
as necessary for publication in that time as are
the great publishing houses to-day.

One other phase of Alcuin's educational activity
remains to be noticed. It is his literary intercourse
with kings and ecclesiastics of influence, touching
the state of learning. Five-sixths of his correspondence, if we may judge by the three hundred
letters now extant, belongs to the eight years which

elapsed between his coming to Tours and his death, and the fulness of information and reminiscence therein preserved is of the first historical value for the latter half of the eighth century. From this rich miscellany it is possible to gather enough information to warrant a judgment as to the fortunes of learning both in Britain and Frankland, with the added advantage of getting many a personal glimpse of the leading actors in the educational movement wherein Alcuin was the central figure.

Some of the letters deal with Britain, for the old man's thoughts turned thither again and again. His first love was his native land, and his home allegiance was never renounced. "Never have I been unfaithful to the people of Britain," he once wrote from the palace of Charles to an Anglo-Saxon presbyter.[1]   And with even more devotion he wrote in the same spirit to his brethren of York shortly before he went to Tours. "My fathers and brethren, dearer than all else in the world, pray do not forget me; for, alike in life and death, I shall ever be yours. And peradventure God in mercy may grant that you, who nursed my infancy, may bury me in old age. But if some other place shall be appointed for my body, yet I believe that my soul will be granted repose among you, through your holy intercession in prayer."[2]

It was perhaps one of his first letters from Tours that was sent to King Offa in response to a request

1 Ep. 15 Jaffé; 8 Migne.
2 Ep. 34 Jaffé; 6 Migne.

that Alcuin should send one of his pupils into Britain to teach. Alcuin complied with Offa's desire, complimenting him on his great zeal for study, — "a zeal so great," he writes, "that the light of learning, though extinguished in many places, now shines in your dominions."[1] To the same year (796) belongs his congratulatory letter to his former pupil, the younger Eanbald, on his elevation to the archbishopric of York. Alcuin gratefully dwells on the fact that it was he who had been privileged to train such a pupil among his "sons" at York. "Praise and glory be to the Lord God Almighty!" he fervently exclaims, "that I, the last of the servants of the Church, was spared to instruct among my sons one who should be held worthy to become a steward of the mysteries of Christ, laboring in my place in the Church wherein I was nursed and instructed, and presiding over the treasures of learning to which my beloved master, Archbishop Ælbert, left me his heir."[2] Then, after general counsels, Alcuin enjoins on his pupil, now archbishop of the see to which he himself would in all probability have been elevated had he remained in England, the duty of keeping up the school. He also tells Eanbald how to conduct it. "Provide masters both for your boys and for the grown-up clerks. Separate into classes those who are to study in books, those who are to practise the church music, and those who

[1] Ep. 43 Jaffé; 49 Migne.
[2] Ep. 72 Jaffé; 56 Migne.

are to engage in transcribing. Have a separate
master for every class, that the boys may not run
about in idleness or occupy themselves in silly play
(*inanes ludos*), or be given over to other follies.
Consider these things most carefully, my dearest
son, to the end that the fountain of all wholesome
erudition may still be found flowing in the chief
city of our nation."[1] It is a strict school that
Alcuin wishes kept. All the play and diversion
for the boys was to be found in their lessons, and
it is evidently Alcuin's old practice as *scholasticus*
at York that is urged upon Eanbald. Yet his
austerity is not morose, and it is noteworthy that
there is neither in this letter nor in any of his
writings a recommendation to use flogging or any
of the other punishments which finally became an
essential part of medieval school discipline. But
for all that, the idea of play was vanity. Still one
can scarcely help thinking that some concession
must have been made by Alcuin to the restless and
sportive nature of boys in his own playful method
of teaching, which verged again and again on
jocoseness and pleasant banter. Another and quite
different point worth noticing is that the principle
of employing a separate master for each subject and
of dividing the pupils into appropriate classes was
practised both at York and Tours, — though at the
palace school it is doubtful whether any such
organization was or could have been effected.

There were other letters sent to Britain. In

[1] Ep. 72 Jaffé; 56 Migne.

one he exhorts Ædilbert, a bishop in Northumbria, to "instruct the youth diligently in the knowledge of books," to keep alive "the light of knowledge" in his diocese, and to bear in mind that "for every one who would understand what to shun and what to pursue, the study of holy books is a necessity." [1] In 797 he writes to the church and people of Canterbury, then distracted by civil and ecclesiastical dissensions, urging them to remember their former renown as a house not only of religion but of "the glory of philosophic study" as well.[2] It was apparently from Tours also that he wrote a general letter of exhortation to the monks of Ireland, in which he bears notable testimony to the Irish learning, with which, of course, he was out of sympathy so far as it encouraged speculative tendencies or departed from the Roman tradition. He recalls how in earlier times many learned masters had come from Ireland into Britain and Gaul, and even into Italy, to the great advantage of the Church. But now the times are perilous, and therefore it behoves them to teach and learn the truth the more zealously, for many false teachers (*pseudodoctores*) have arisen, introducing new and unheard-of opinions, and bent on getting glory for themselves by their novel teachings. "Therefore, most holy fathers, exhort your youth to learn the traditions of the catholic doctors." "However,"

[1] Ep. 88 Jaffé; 178 Migne. The date of this letter is uncertain and may be earlier than Alcuin's removal to Tours.
[2] Ep. 86 Jaffé; 74 Migne.

he pointedly remarks, "the study of secular letters
is not to be set aside.   Let grammar stand as the
fundamental study for the tender years of infancy
and the other disciplines of philosophical subtlety
be regarded as the several ascents of learning by
which scholars may mount to the very summit of
evangelical perfection.   Thus with their increase
of years there shall come an increase of the riches
of wisdom." [1]

His correspondence in Frankland was meanwhile
assiduously kept up, and in this way he was able to
watch from Tours the course of affairs throughout
the kingdom.   The interests of the palace school
engaged his attention, though he had ceased to
be its master, and the condition of education in
general likewise continued to be a matter of constant concern, though Theodulf had virtually taken
his place as soon as he removed to Tours.

His congratulations to Theodulf as the new minister of education, or "father of the vineyards," as
Alcuin fancifully styles him, are embodied in what
is probably the most variegated piece of allegorical
scriptural patchwork he ever composed.   It defies
adequate reproduction in English, unless accompanied with a separate note of explanation for
almost every line.   However, it is a letter of such
distinct importance as to need presentation at least
in part; for its playful vagaries contain not only
Alcuin's congratulations, but his injunctions to
Theodulf to promote the study of the old seven

[1] Ep. 217 Jaffé; 225 Migne.

liberal arts without any admixture of new notions. The "vineyards" of the letter are the educational interests of the kingdom.   The "wine cellars" are the stores of learning in general, and the "old wine" or the "good wine which has been kept until now" is the excellent wine of the liberal arts, "kept until now" to be broached in the age of Charles. This is the true feast of both bread and wine to which Wisdom or *Sapientia* invites her followers in the ninth chapter of Proverbs, as Alcuin explains in another letter, "the true wine which she mingles for those that are bidden to her table which is spread in the house she hath builded on seven pillars." [1]

With this preface we are prepared for a simplified version of part of Alcuin's letter to Theodulf.   It opens as follows:

"Albinus wisheth health to Theodulf, the great prelate and father of the vineyards.

"We read in the Book of Chronicles that in the time of David, the king after God's own heart, Zabdi was set 'over the king's wine cellars.' [2] Now, by the mercy of God, a second David is the ruler of a better people, and under him a nobler Zabdi is set over the cellars; for the king hath set his love upon him and 'brought him into the wine-cellars,' [3] that the scholars may there wreathe him with flowers and 'comfort him with the flagons' [4] of that 'wine which maketh glad the heart of man.' [5]

---

[1] Ep. 292 Jaffé; 185 Migne.   [4] Solomon's Song ii 5.
[2] I Chronicles xxvii 27.   [5] Psalm civ 15.
[3] Solomon's Song ii 4.

"So then, even if there be lacking 'bread which strengtheneth man's heart,'[1] yet there is not lacking in the cellars of Orleans the wine which maketh glad, for our hope is in the fruitful vine, and not in any withered fig-tree.[2] Wherefore I, the new Jonathan, 'counsellor of our David and his man of letters,'[3] send this letter unto Zabdi, saying: Let us arise early and see how fairly the vine flourishes in 'the valley of Sorek';[4] let us 'tread out the wine-press with shouting,'[5] that the streams of the wine-cellar may be dispersed abroad."[6]

Thus this fanciful commingling of serious and playful exhortation in regard to Theodulf's duties to the "vineyards" and "wine-presses" of learning proceeds, changing for a moment at the close of the letter into apparent remonstrance. "Say not, 'I cannot rise, and give thee,'[7] for even if thou hast not 'three loaves'[8] of bread to lend, yet by the blessing of Christ there at hand are 'the seven waterpots'[9] full of the 'good wine which has been kept until now,'[10] and kept, as all know, to be mingled by 'the ruler of the feast'[11] who dwells in Tours. Therefore let the old wine still be kept, in order that no one may put 'new wine into the old

[1] Psalm civ 15.
[2] Matthew xxi 19.
[3] I Chronicles xxvii 32. This is Jonathan, the uncle of David.
[4] Judges xvi 4.
[5] Jeremiah xlviii 33.
[6] Proverbs v 16.
[7] Luke xi 7
[8] Luke xi 5.
[9] John ii 6–7. Alcuin must have his 'seven waterpots' for the liberal arts, though there are only six in Scripture.
[10] John ii 10.
[11] John ii 9.

bottles,'[1] for 'no man having drunk old wine
straightway desireth new; for he saith: The old
is better.'[2]

"Happy is he that speaketh to one that hath ears
to hear. Farewell, my dearest brother."[3]

This is no ordinary letter; for it is as far removed
from the simplicity of style which often shows
itself in Alcuin's writing as from the labored
manner of his more learned discourses. It is
a conscious attempt at an artificial manner of
letter-writing, sometimes affected by scholars in
that age, and is intended to gather together and
display such allegorical hints of Scripture as might
bear in favor of promoting the liberal arts; and
what could be more convincing as argument than
allegory? We may be sure that Theodulf had
"ears to hear" and to heed its teachings; for the
"paraphrastical" and "paradigmatic" epistolary
touches[4] in which it abounds, and which were so
dear to Alcuin, would be fully understood by
Theodulf, who might well regard them as highly
complimentary to his powers of literary apprecia-
tion. The exhortation to prefer the "old wine,"
which Alcuin had mingled as "ruler of the feast,"
to any "new wine" that might be offered, was
unnecessary in one respect, for Theodulf showed
himself a vigorous supporter of the teachings of
his master. Yet the caution was timely; for new
teachers were appearing at the palace of Charles,

[1] Luke v 37.   [3] Ep. 153 Jaffé; 148 Migne.
[2] Luke v 39.   [4] Ep. 177 Jaffé; 191 Migne.

introducing strange notions, which were incompat-
ible with the teachings of Alcuin. These were
certain Irish scholars who inculcated, among other
things, a mode of calculating Easter different from
the tradition of Rome, and akin to that followed in
the eastern Church. At first sight this seems too
slight a matter to arouse comment, but the calculation of Easter was one of the questions upon which
the East and West were hopelessly divided. Though
not a capital question in itself, it was one of great
strategic importance as a test of ecclesiastical loyalty. It had a similar importance in relation to the
tradition of learning as delivered by Cassiodorus,
Isidore, and Bede, — all faithful Latins; for with
their doctrine of Easter the Irish scholars coupled
other teachings, and no doubt brought with them
the odious book of Martianus Capella, — and who
knows what Greek books they may not likewise
have brought with them? It is the irrepressible
conflict of tradition with speculation that is setting
in. Alcuin wrote again and again to Charles, argu-
ing for the Roman method of calculating Easter
and lamenting that such dark "Egyptian" teachings should have drifted in to blind the youth at
the palace. Theodulf also wrote a satirical poem,
setting forth the utter perverseness and worth-
lessness of the self-confident "*Scotellus,*" or Irish
scholar. Charles, however, viewed the situation
more cheerfully and sought to draw Alcuin into
debate with the *Scotelli*, perhaps hoping for no
small enjoyment from witnessing the contest. But

Alcuin preferred to stay at Tours. He was in no mood to be humiliated at the palace in his old age, and so he informs the king that "the aged Entellus has long since laid aside the cestus, and left it for others who are younger."[1] "Of what avail," he exclaims, "would be the feebleness of your Flaccus amid the clash of arms? What can the timid hare do against the wild boars, or the lamb among the lions?"[2] Still he does not conceal his annoyance or his surprise that such foolish teachings should have been given any audience. As for himself, he says, "These silly little questions beset my ears like the insects that swarm at the windows in summer,"[3] and therefore he expresses great surprise that Charles should have listened to them, and exhorts him to summon to his side able defenders of the faith, lest this latest heresy spread to the distraction of the Church and his own kingdom.[4]

Next after Charles, his chief correspondent was his beloved friend Arno, archbishop of Salzburg, whom he did not fail to advise as to the care of all the parishes in his diocese, insisting that there should be a general establishment of primary schools, wherein the elements should be faithfully taught.[5] In one letter, he ventures out of his depth into metaphysics, and attempts to explain to Arno the distinction between the terms "substance,"

[1] Ep. 98, p. 408 Jaffé; 82 Migne.
[2] Ep. 98, p. 412 Jaffé; 82 Migne.
[3] Ep. 96, p. 398 Jaffé; 80 Migne.
[4] Ep. 99, p. 420 Jaffé; 83 Migne.
[5] Ep. 91 Jaffé; 94 Migne.

"essence," "subsistence," and "nature." But he
was not a philosopher, and his observations on
"essence" are enough to establish this fact.
"Essence," he says, "is properly spoken of with
reference to God, he who always is what he is,
and who said unto Moses, 'I am that I am.' Now,
God alone truly is, inasmuch as he is unchangeable; for of whatsoever is changeable we cannot
say that it truly is in every respect, because it can
become what it is not, and hence not be what it
is." [1] In still another letter he justifies to Arno
the reading of the classical poets, quoting Jerome
to support him. After citing Jerome's saying,
"Even the gold which is found on the dunghill
is to be prized and to be deposited in the Lord's
treasury," he adds by way of comment: "It was
the blessed apostle Paul himself who found the
gold of wisdom in the dung of the poets, and
transferred it to the treasury of ecclesiastical learning, and so have all the holy doctors done, who were
instructed after his example." [2] It seems strange
after such a letter to find Alcuin's attitude so ascetic
in his last years towards the poet Virgil. [3] In his boyhood he loved to read Virgil more than he did the
Latin Psalms, and his own poetry, both in respect to
metre and diction, is largely drawn from the same
source. Yet he afterwards told his pupils that the
poetry of the Bible was sufficient for them, and

[1] Ep. 209 Jaffé; 161 Migne.
[2] Ep. 147 Jaffé; 117 Migne.
[3] *Monumenta Alcuiniana*, p. 6.

that they should run no risks from the effeminating
verses of Virgil.   Once Sigulf had ventured to read
his Virgil secretly, contrary to Alcuin's injunction,
and when Alcuin discovered it he overwhelmed
him with the alarming question, "How now! Vir-
gilian!   Why is it that against my advice, and
apart from my knowledge, you have desired to read
Virgil?"   Sigulf cast himself at Alcuin's feet in
abject penitence.   His master reproved him aus-
terely, but finally forgave him, adding his caution
never to do so any more.[1]   Even Rigbod, though
archbishop of Treves, did not escape his reproof.
"Has the love of Virgil," he complains, "taken
away all remembrance of me?   Oh! that my name
were Virgil!   Then indeed should I be ever before
your eyes, and you would ponder my words with
deep regard.   But Flaccus is gone, and Virgil has
come.   Oh! that the four Gospels and not the
twelve Æneads might fill your thoughts!"[2]   As
for himself, when he sends to Rigbod for books, he
begs for very different reading; namely, a Homily
of St. Leo and a treatise of the Venerable Bede on
the Book of Tobias.[3]

Alcuin's seclusion at Tours was broken by a visit
from Charles.   In the spring of 800[4] the king had
tarried some days at the monastery, in company

[1] *Monumenta Alcuiniana*, pp. 24, 25.

[2] Ep. 216 Jaffé; 169 Migne.   Alcuin's "Aeneads" for
"Aeneïds" is only too characteristic of the decadent state of
Latin in his time.

[3] Ep. 197 Jaffé; 171 Migne.

[4] Ep. 133, Note 1, Jaffé; 103 Migne.

with his Queen Liutgard, whose health was rapidly
failing. She died there early in June of the same
year and was buried in the adjoining church.
Charles himself returned in the same month to
Aachen by way of Orleans and Paris, accompanied
by Alcuin,[1] who left his monastic retreat for a
short time in order to hold a public dispute with
Felix of Urgel regarding the Adoptionist heresy.
In this discussion Felix acknowledged himself
completely vanquished by Alcuin's arguments.

As the autumn approached, Charles prepared to
go to Rome. Alcuin had been invited to make the
journey with him. But the infirmities of age,
which were daily growing upon him, coupled with
his instinctive aversion to participating in political
affairs, except as a peacemaker, kept him at Tours.
Charles went to Rome, and on Christmas day was
crowned Emperor of the Holy Roman Empire by
Pope Leo, thus establishing the foundations of
social order for the middle ages. There is abundant evidence for supposing that Charles suspected
the Pope's intentions, though not apprised of the
time or occasion when they were to be carried into
effect. It is also quite evident that Alcuin was
aware of the significance of this journey to Rome,
and perhaps it is not too much to say that he had
secretly advised it, and by his correspondence with
Rome was influential in bringing about the corona-
tion. When Charles returned from Rome to Aachen
as Emperor, Alcuin made it his first care to send

[1] Ep. 147, p. 558, Note 1, Jaffé; 117 Migne.

to him by a messenger a superbly written copy of
the Gospels, made at the monastery in Tours, as
the worthiest contribution he could offer to the
"splendor of the imperial power." [1]

As Alcuin's end drew near, he set in order all
his affairs, naming his pupil Fridugis as his successor at Tours. A year or more before his
death he wrote a letter to Charles, bidding him
farewell, invoking manifold blessings upon him
for all his goodness, and reminding him of the
supreme importance of preparation for death and
the day of judgment. [2] Other letters written about
the same time show how wholly his mind was
engrossed with the thought of his coming departure. The opening of the year 804 found him
greatly weakened in health. A fever soon set
in, under which his remaining strength gradually
ebbed away. It was his desire that he might
linger until the day of Pentecost should come.
And so it happened; for Alcuin died at dawn of
that May morning, [3] just after matins had been
sung.

He was carried to his burial in the church of St.
Martin, near the monastery, with every manifestation of reverence and affection. It was a fitting
place for his repose. Notwithstanding his cherished hope that it might be his lot to die and
be buried at York, his works which followed him

[1] Ep. 205 Jaffé; 131 Migne.
[2] Ep. 193 Jaffé; 134 Migne.
[3] May 19, 804.

were chiefly his labors in Frankland, and in Frankland Tours was the scene of his last, and in some
ways his greatest service. It was also a spot where
other appropriate memories clustered. There St.
Martin had come as a founder of monasticism among
the Gauls. There Charles Martel had delivered the
Frank from the Moslem. Thither Charles the Great
had journeyed to take counsel with Alcuin before
he went to Rome, to return as monarch of the Holy
Roman Empire. There his best beloved queen,
Liutgard, the devoted friend of Alcuin, had died
and was buried; and there, too, if the tradition
be true, Alcuin pointed out to Charles the young
prince Lewis as his successor.

And yet, when the news of his death was borne to
distant York, and the brethren there were chanting
prayers for his repose, they might easily believe
his longing desire that his soul might rest among
them, wherever his body lay, was then being fulfilled.

CHAPTER V

THE EDUCATIONAL WRITINGS OF ALCUIN

ALCUIN's writings have been preserved to us in tolerable completeness, and may be classified under a fourfold division. First come his theological works, which embrace the greater part, perhaps two-thirds, of all that he wrote. This theological portion may in turn be divided into four parts, exegetical, dogmatic, liturgical and practical, and lives of the saints. Of the remaining third of his writings, the major part is embraced in his epistles, and least in extent are the didactic treatises and poems which make up the rest.

It will thus be seen that the greater part of Alcuin's writings have little connection with the history of education, and yet, even his theological works have incidental interest in this respect. Besides a few scanty gleanings from his exegetical writings, there are two of his practical treatises, *On the Virtues and Vices* and *On the Nature of the Soul*, which have a general connection with education, but beyond this there is nothing to be found. The epistles are of high value for the general history of the times, and more particularly for the abundant light which they shed upon the activity of Alcuin in his relation to the restoration of school-learning. The poems have a lesser value, but contain important help for the history of the school at York, where Alcuin was bred, and for his later career in Frankland. But the chief interest centres in his specifically didactic writings, for they contain most fully his general views on education as well as separate treatises on some of the liberal arts.

Let it be remarked at the outset that Alcuin is rarely an original writer, but usually a compiler and adapter, and even at times a literal transcriber of other men's work. He adds nothing to the sum of learning, either by invention or by recovery of what has been lost. What he does is to reproduce or adapt from earlier authors such parts of their writings as could be appreciated by the age in which he lived. Accordingly, while he must be refused all the credit that belongs to a courageous mind which advances beyond what has been known, he must yet be highly esteemed for the invaluable service he rendered as a transmitter and conserver of the learning that was in danger of perishing, and as the restorer and propagator of this learning in a great empire, after it had been extinct for generations. A passage from the letter dedicating his commentary on the Gospel of John to Gisela and Rotrud, states so aptly the timorously conservative attitude which appears in all his literary efforts, educational or otherwise, that it is worth citing here. He writes: "I have reverently traversed the store-houses of the early fathers, and whatever I have been able to find there, I have sent of it for you to taste. First of all, I have sought help from St. Augustine, who has devoted the greatest study to expounding the most holy words of this holy gospel. Next, I have drawn somewhat from the lesser works of St. Ambrose, that most holy doctor, and likewise from the Homilies of the distinguished father, Gregory the Great. I have also taken much from the Homilies of the blessed presbyter Bede, and from other holy fathers, whose interpretations I have here set forth. For I have preferred to employ their thoughts and words rather than to venture anything of my own audacity, even if the curiosity of my readers were to approve of it, and by a most cautious manner of writing I have made it my care, with the help of God, not to set down anything contrary to the thoughts of the fathers."

Fortunately for his theological works, he depends mainly on the really great fathers of the Latin Church. Most of what he writes comes from Augustine, Jerome, Ambrose and Gregory the Great, while Bede is the chief of his later authorities. Of the Greek fathers, however, he knows nothing, except through Latin versions, and of these he makes no considerable use beyond drawing on a translation of Chrysostom to help in composing his commentary on the Epistle to the Hebrews. His literary sources are all Latin, nor is there any Greek to be found in what he wrote, apart from some citations copied from Jerome and occasional Greek words from elsewhere. On the educational

side he depends mainly on Isidore and Bede, but
with subsidiary help from Cassiodorus and the treatise *On the Categories* falsely ascribed to Augustine.
He knew of Boethius, but made only indirect use
of him.   Martianus Capella is not so much as mentioned.

The separate educational treatises of Alcuin of
undoubtedly genuine character are the following:
*On Grammar, On Orthography, On Rhetoric and the
Virtues, On Dialectics*, a *Disputation with Pepin*, and
a tedious astronomical treatise, entitled *De Cursu et
Saltu Lunœ ac Bissexto*.   Three others are ascribed
to him with less certainty: *On the Seven Arts, A
Disputation for Boys*, and the so-called *Propositions
of Alcuin*.

First and most important of these is his *Grammar*, which falls into two parts, the one a dialogue
between Alcuin and his pupils on philosophy and
liberal studies in general, and the other a dialogue between a young Saxon and a Frank on
grammar, also conducted in the presence of Alcuin.
The former dialogue is an original composition
and contains in brief compass Alcuin's views on
the end and method of education, and on the duty
of studying the liberal arts, to which the entire
dialogue serves as a general introduction.   "Most
learned master," says one of the disciples, opening
the dialogue, "we have often heard you say that
Philosophy was the mistress of all the virtues,
and alone of all earthly riches never made its
possessor miserable.   We confess that you have

incited us by such words to follow after this excellent felicity, and we desire to know what is the sum of its supremacy and by what steps we may make ascent thereunto. Our age is yet a tender one and too weak to rise unhelped by your hand. We know, indeed, that the strength of the mind is in the heart, as the strength of the eyes is in the head. Now our eyes, whenever they are flooded by the splendor of the sun, or by reason of the presence of any light, are able to discern most clearly whatever is presented to their gaze, but without this access of light they must remain in darkness. So also the mind is able to receive wisdom if there be any one who will enlighten it." Alcuin benignantly replies, " My sons, ye have said well in comparing the eyes to the mind, and may the light that lighteneth every man that cometh into this world enlighten your minds, to the end that ye may be able to make progress in philosophy, which, as ye have well said, never deserts its possessor." The disciples assent to this and then renew their entreaty in the same figurative and flowery manner. " Verily, Master," they urge, "we know that we must ask of Him who giveth liberally and upbraideth not. Yet we likewise need to be instructed slowly, with many a pause and hesitation, and like the weak and feeble to be led by slow steps until our strength shall grow. The flint naturally contains in itself the fire that will come forth when the flint is struck. Even so there is in the human mind the light of knowledge that will remain hidden like the spark in the flint, unless it be brought forth by the repeated efforts of a teacher." Alcuin answers: "It is easy indeed to point out to you the path of wisdom, if only ye love it for the sake of God, for knowledge, for purity of heart, for understanding the truth, yea, and for itself. Seek it not to gain the praise of men or the honors of this world, nor yet for the deceitful pleasures of riches, for the more these things are loved, so much the farther do they cause those who seek them to depart from the light of truth and knowledge."

After this elaborately courteous opening the dialogue proceeds to show that true and eternal happiness, and not transitory pleasure, is the proper end for a rational being to set before him, and that this happiness consists in the things that are proper and peculiar to the soul itself, rather than in what is alien to it. "That," says Alcuin, "which is sought from without is alien to the soul, as is the gathering together of riches, but that which is proper to the soul is what is within, namely, the graces of wisdom. Therefore, O man," he calls out in fervid apostrophe, "if thou art master of thyself, thou shalt have what thou shalt never have to grieve at losing, and what no calamity shall be able to take away. Why then, O mortals, do ye seek without for that which ye have within? How much better is it to be adorned within than without!" "What, then, are the adornments of the soul?" the disciples naturally inquire, and Alcuin answers:

"Wisdom is the chief adornment, and this I urge you to seek above all things."

Alcuin then explains that wisdom is itself eternal because it is an inseparable property of the soul, which is immortal, and in this differs from everything else of a secular character. But its pursuit is laborious. The scholar will not gain his reward without study, any more than the soldier without fighting or the farmer without plowing. It is an old proverb that the root of learning is bitter but the fruit is sweet, and so St. Paul asserts that "every discipline at the present is not joyous but grievous, yet afterwards it yieldeth the peaceable fruit of righteousness to them that were exercised in it." Progress in secular knowledge is to be made by slow ascents, step by step, and is to lead to "the better ways of wisdom, which conduct to life eternal." "May the divine grace guide and lead us," exclaims Alcuin, "into the treasures of spiritual wisdom, that ye may be intoxicated at the fountain of divine plenty; that there may be within you a well of water springing up unto everlasting life. But, inasmuch as the Apostle enjoins that everything be done decently and in order, I think that ye should be led by the steps of erudition from lower to higher things until your wings gradually grow stronger, so that ye may mount on them to view the loftier visions of the pure ether." The disciples are overwhelmed and humbly answer: "Master, raise us from the earth by your hand and set our feet upon the ascents of wisdom."

Alcuin accordingly proceeds to set before his pupils the seven ascents of the liberal arts in the following manner: "We have read how Wisdom herself saith by the mouth of Solomon, 'Wisdom hath builded her house, she hath hewn out her seven pillars.' Now although this saying pertains to the Divine Wisdom which builded for Himself a house (that is, the body of Christ in the Virgin's womb), and endued it with the seven gifts of the Holy Ghost, or may mean the Church, which is the House of God that shines with these gifts, yet Wisdom is also built upon the seven pillars of liberal letters, and it can in no wise afford us access to any perfect knowledge, unless it be set upon these seven pillars, or ascents." Here is a distinct advance on Alcuin's part beyond the earlier writers on the liberal arts. Augustine had regarded them with qualified approval because they were helpful towards understanding divine truth. Cassiodorus saw in addition a mystical hint of their excellence in the fact that they were seven, and fortified his position by the text, "Wisdom hath builded her house, she hath hewn out her seven columns." Alcuin takes up the text from Proverbs quoted by Cassiodorus, and finds in it the liberal arts as a matter of direct interpretation. *Sapientia*, or Wisdom, who had builded her house and hewn out her seven pillars, he mystically explains first of Christ the Divine Wisdom and next of the Church, each endued with the seven gifts of the Spirit, and then proceeds to his third application, which is that

Sapientia, or Wisdom, which in the speech of his time often meant learning, was built upon the seven liberal arts. Augustine found the arts outside of Scripture, but deemed them helpful towards understanding it. Cassiodorus found in Scripture a mystical hint as to their excellence, and Alcuin gets them out of Scripture itself. It needs not to be told how influential such an interpretation would be on the fortunes of secular learning; for if the arts were once found in the Scriptures, there was no way of getting them out of the Church. Henceforth the proscriptive utterances of Tertullian, though echoed once and again down the middle ages,[1] could never dominate the Church.

But let us return to the dialogue. The pupils renew their request: "Open to us, as you have often promised, the seven ascents of theoretical discipline." Alcuin replies: "Here, then, are the ascents of which ye are in search, and O that ye may ever be as eager to ascend them as ye now are to see them. They are grammar, rhetoric, dialectics, arithmetic, geometry, music, and astrology. On these the philosophers bestowed their leisure and their study." Then he adds with a boldness which might well have alarmed him: "By reason of these philosophers the catholic teachers and defenders of our faith have proved themselves

---

[1] As late as the thirteenth century we read in a regulation of the Dominican order: "*In libris gentilium philosophorum non studeat, et si ad horam suscipiat saeculares scientias, non addiscat, nec artes quas liberales vocant.*"

superior to all the chief heretics in public controversy," and closes with the exhortation: " Let your
youthful steps, my dearest sons, run daily along
these paths until a riper age and a stronger mind
shall bring you to the heights of Holy Scripture."

Plainly in Alcuin's mind the arts were seven
and only seven. They are the necessary ascents
to the higher wisdom of the Scriptures. Not the
fact that they are simply useful to the Scriptures,
but indispensable, is what gives them such value
in Alcuin's eyes. Much of the rhetoric in which
his ideas exfoliate is childish enough, but it is
impossible not to see behind it all a pure and gentle
spirit, who valued the scanty sum of learning he
possessed for no lesser reasons than the love of
God, purity of soul, knowledge of truth, and even
for its own sake, as against any pursuit of learning for the vulgar ends of wealth, popularity or
secular honor.

The second dialogue in the treatise is properly
grammatical. Two of Alcuin's pupils, a Saxon
and a Frank, are beginners in the study, or, to put
it in Alcuin's flowery language, "They but lately
rushed upon the thorny thickets of grammatical
density." The Frank is a boy of fourteen years
and the Saxon of fifteen. The master presides
over their interrogations and answers. It is decided
that grammar must begin with the consideration of
what a letter is, though Alcuin stops on the way to
expound the nature of words. It is defined as
"the least part of an articulate sound." The letters

are the "elements" of language because they are
ultimate and indivisible, and are built up first into
syllables, and thereafter successively into words,
clauses, and sentences. Letters are of two sorts,
vowels and consonants, and are defined as follows:
"The vowels are uttered by themselves and of
themselves make syllables. The consonants cannot be uttered by themselves, nor can they of themselves make syllables." But this sapient definition
by antithesis, though accepted by the pupils, does
not contain all that is to be said. There is an occult
reason why the alphabet is divided into vowels and
consonants, as Alcuin at once informs them. "The
vowels," he says, "are, as it were, the souls, and
the consonants, the bodies of words." "Now the
soul moves both itself and the body, but the body
is immovable apart from the soul. Such, then, are
the consonants without the vowels. They may
indeed be written by themselves, but they can
neither be uttered nor have any power apart from
vowels." This explanation seems to satisfy them,
for they pursue the matter no further. The peculiarities of the consonants are then discussed very
much in the same manner, and the syllable is next
taken up. It is defined as "a sound expressed in letters (*vox litteralis*), which has been uttered with one
accent and at one breath." The discussion of syllables falls into four parts, accent (*accentus*), breath-
ings (*spiritus*), quantity (*tempus*), and the number of
constituent letters. After these are discussed, the
pupils entreat that before proceeding further they

may be furnished with a definition of grammar. Alcuin accordingly tells them that "Grammar is the science of written sounds (*litteralis scientia*), the guardian of correct speaking and writing. It is founded on nature, reason, authority, and custom." It has been well observed that this shrunken notion of grammar on the part of Alcuin as contrasted with the wide conception of the study that prevailed among the grammarians of the later Roman Empire is thoroughly characteristic of the intellectual feebleness of the later time. Instead of being both the art of writing and speaking, and also the study of the great poets and orators, it has now become only the former of these, a childish, technical and barren study. This appears more plainly as we advance to Alcuin's alarming enumeration of the parts of grammar. They are "words, letters, syllables, clauses, sayings, speeches, definitions, feet, accents, punctuation marks, critical marks, orthographies, analogies, etymologies, glosses, distinctions, barbarisms, solecisms, faults, metaplasms, figurations, tropes, prose, metres, fables, and histories."

Words, letters and syllables, the first three of Alcuin's twenty-six parts of grammar, have been discussed, and each of the others is next defined. Alcuin then proceeds to the consideration of the different parts of speech in the following order: the noun, its genders, numbers, "figures" and cases; the pronoun, its genders, "figures," numbers and cases; then the verb with its modes, "figures," inflections and numbers; and the adverb with its "figures." Lastly he treats of the participle, the conjunction, the preposition and the interjection. By "figures" Alcuin means the facts relating to the simplicity, composition or derivation of words. Thus, under his "figures" of verbs, the word *cupio* is in simple figure, *concupio* is in composite figure, and *concupisco* is in derivative figure, because it comes from *concupio*. The whole treatment of the parts of speech is similarly feeble in spirit and almost entirely restricted to etymology, so that Alcuin's *Grammar* is really devoid of orthography, syntax and prosody. Whatever is excellent in any way in his *Grammar* ought to be credited to Donatus, whom Alcuin follows. Isidore also furnishes him many a definition, but wherever this happens the treatise is apt to be childish. An example or two may suffice. The derivation of *littera* is said to be from *legitera*, "because the *littera* prepares a path for readers (*leg entibus iter*)." Feet in poetry are so named "because the metres walk on them," and so on. Yet his book had great fame, and Notker, writing a century later, praised it, saying, "Alcuin has made such a grammar that Donatus, Nicomachus, Dositheus and our own Priscian seem as nothing when compared with him."

In the manuscript copies of the *Grammar* there appear to be some slight parts missing at the end, so that it may have been more extended than we suppose; but there is no ground for thinking it

covered more than etymology.   However, Alcuin's
next work is on orthography, and is properly a
pendant to his *Grammar*.   It is a short manual
containing a list of words, alphabetically arranged,
with comments on their proper spelling, pronunciation and meanings, and with remarks on their
correct use, drawn to some extent from a treatise
by Bede on the same subject.   It is a sort of
Antibarbarus, a help towards securing accuracy
of form and propriety of use in the employment of
Latin words, and must have been serviceable in
the instruction of youth, but more so in the copying of ancient manuscripts.   We may reasonably
believe that Alcuin's scribes in the monastery
of Tours, busily engaged in recovering one and
another patristic and classical writer, were guided
by his book in the purification of the copies they
made, and for which the monastery at Tours became so famous.   "Let him who would publish
the sayings of the ancients read me, for he who
follows me not will speak without regard to
law,"[1] is the translation of the couplet which
stands at the head of the *Orthography* and indicates its purpose.   It is Alcuin's attempt to purge
contemporary Latin of its barbarisms.   He puts
his comments oddly enough.   "Write *vinea*," he
says, "if you mean a vine, with *i* in the first
syllable and *e* in the second.   But if you mean
pardon, write *venia* with *e* in the first syllable and

---

[1] Me legat antiquas vult qui proferre loquelas.
Me qui non sequitur, vult sine lege loqui.

i in the second. Write *vacca* with a *v*, if you mean a cow, but write it with a *b* if you mean a berry." In the same way be careful to write *vellus* with a *v* to mean wool, and *bellus*, if you mean fair. Similarly, when writing, do not confuse *vel* with *fel* which means gall, or with *Bel*, the heathen god. By no means consider *benificus*, a man of good deeds, the same as *venificus*, a poisoner. So *bibo* and *vivo* are not to be mixed. Such examples indicate that Alcuin had to struggle against "rusticity" in pronunciation as well as in writing, — a rusticity which was due to the modifying influence of the barbarous Tudesque upon the pronouncing of Latin, — an influence which, even in Alcuin's time, was altering the forms of words in a manner which presaged the final demolition of Latin prior to the rise of French.

Some of the definitions are quite amusing. *Coelebs*, a bachelor, is defined as "one who is on his way *ad coelum*," evidently the true monk. "Write *aequor* with a diphthong," for the reason that it is derived from *aqua*. *Mālus*, a mast, is to have a long *a*, but "a *mălus homo* ought to have a short *a*."

It is on the *Grammar* and *Orthography* that Alcuin's didactic fame principally rests, and justly so, for in spite of their puerile character they did more good service than anything else he wrote. Let it be remembered that the tall, blue-eyed barbarians, whom Alcuin was aiming to civilize, were but little children when it came to school-learning. Let it also be remembered that Alcuin, divesting himself

of all vanity and conceit, wisely and even humbly
set before them what they could learn, and the
only thing they could learn at the start. Even
his master, Charles, had to toil painfully to bend
his fingers, stiffened with long use of the sword, to
the clerkly task of writing, and confessed that he
acquired the art with great difficulty.

The dialogue *On Rhetoric and the Virtues* has
for its two interlocutors Charles and Alcuin, and
was composed in response to a request from the
king. Alcuin instructs him in the elements of
the rhetorical art with special reference to its
applications in the conduct and settlement of dis-
putes in civil affairs, and closes with a short description of the four cardinal virtues, — prudence,
justice, fortitude and temperance. It is, therefore, not strictly a book on rhetoric, but rather on
its applications. It is based on rhetorical writings of Cicero, which are rehandled by Alcuin,
and always with loss and injury to his originals.
The hand of Isidore is likewise visible in places,
and contributes to the general deterioration. If
the *Grammar* was rudimentary and ill-arranged,
the *Rhetoric* suffers yet more from its miscellaneous
presentation of ill-digested bits of rhetoric, and
from its greater dulness of style. Moreover, it is
less jocose in spirit than are parts of the *Grammar*,
though Alcuin's specimen of sophistical reasoning,
which he produces for the instruction of the king,
is indeed comical. "What art thou?" asks Alcuin,
and after Charles answers, "I am a man (*homo*),"
the dialogue goes on as follows: —

"*Alcuin.* See how thou hast shut me in.

Charles. How so?

Alcuin. If thou sayest I am not the same as thou, and that I am a man, it follows that thou art not a man.

Charles. It does.

Alcuin. But how many syllables has *homo?*

Charles. Two.

Alcuin. Then art thou those two syllables?

Charles. Surely not; but why dost thou reason thus?

Alcuin. That thou mayest understand sophistical craft and see how thou canst be forced to a conclusion.

Charles. I see and understand from what was granted at the start, both that I am *homo* and that *homo* has two syllables, and that I can be shut up to the conclusion that I am these two syllables. But I wonder at the subtlety with which thou hast led me on, first to conclude that thou wert not a man, and afterward of myself, that I was two syllables."

After the *Rhetoric* comes the *Dialectics*, which is in part extracted or abridged from Isidore, who in his turn had taken from Boethius, and in part copied almost solidly from the supposed work of Augustine on the *Categories* of Aristotle. If possible, it is less original than the *Rhetoric*, but is at least what its title indicates, — an attempt to say something about dialectics. However, as the age of medieval logic had not yet begun in earnest,

Alcuin's treatise was perhaps as much as the times would bear, especially in view of the existing indifference or antagonism in the Church to the subtleties of Aristotle. In conjunction with the *Grammar* and *Rhetoric*, it may be taken as constituting such instruction in the *trivium* as was given in the palace school.

Interesting in its way as a specimen of Alcuin's teaching is his dialogue written for Pepin, then a young prince of sixteen years, and entitled *The Disputation of Pepin, the Most Noble and Royal Youth, with Albinus the Scholastic.* It rambles without plan and allegorizes without restraint. Parts of it run as follows: —

"*Pepin.* What is writing?

Albinus. The guardian of history.

Pepin. What is language?

Albinus. The betrayer of the soul.

Pepin. What generates language?

Albinus. The tongue.

Pepin. What is the tongue?

Albinus. The whip of the air.

Pepin. What is air?

Albinus. The guardian of life.

Pepin. What is life?

Albinus. The joy of the happy; the expectation of death.

Pepin. What is death?

Albinus. An inevitable event; an uncertain journey; tears for the living; the probation of wills; the stealer of men.

Pepin. What is man?

Albinus. The slave of death; a passing traveler; a stranger in his place.

Pepin. What is man like?

Albinus. An apple."

Let us understand this short and sudden definition. Alcuin means that man hangs like an apple on a tree without being able to know when he is to fall.

The questions on natural phenomena are not less instructive: —

"*Pepin.* What is water?

Albinus. A supporter of life; a cleanser of filth.

Pepin. What is fire?

Albinus. Excessive heat; the nurse of growing things; the ripener of crops.

Pepin. What is cold?

Albinus. The febricity of our members.[1]

Pepin. What is frost?

Albinus. The persecutor of plants; the destruction of leaves; the bond of the earth; the source of waters.

Pepin. What is snow?

Albinus. Dry water.

Pepin. What is the winter?

Albinus. The exile of summer.

Pepin. What is the spring?

Albinus. The painter of the earth.

Pepin. What is the autumn?

Albinus. The barn of the year."

[1] This " cold " is apparently a chill.

After more of this same sort, the dialogue rapidly runs into puzzles and then closes.

The treatise *De Cursu et Saltu Lunæ ac Bissexto* needs no special notice. It deals with the method of calculating the changes of the moon with special reference to the determination of Easter, and is compiled for the instruction of the king. Bede is the principal authority.

There remain for consideration the three works somewhat doubtfully attributed to Alcuin. The first is entitled *On the Seven Arts,* and is a fragment derived from the work of Cassiodorus on the same subject. But only the first two parts, grammar and rhetoric, are described, and they are in part copied and in part abridged from their original. Alcuin may have taken them after his manner from Cassiodorus, without any thought of laying claim to the production as his own. But whether he did this or not, the fragment is useful in that it shows that the book of Cassiodorus *On the Arts and Disciplines of Liberal Letters* was consulted in the time of Alcuin. The so-called *Disputation of the Boys* is likewise doubtful. It is a set of questions and answers on Scriptural subjects and may at least serve as another example of the catechetical method of that time. Much more interesting is the set of puzzles entitled *The Propositions of Alcuin, the Teacher of the Emperor Charles the Great, for Whetting the Wit of Youth.* Unfortunately, the Venerable Bede had written just such a treatise, which is here closely copied. But this need not weigh against the probability of Alcuin's taking and using it. But whether he did really do so, or whether copyists attributed it to him, is a matter of little moment, for it well represents the character of the teaching of the time. It is, in fact, not unlikely that these are the propositions which Alcuin enclosed in a letter to Charles and styled "certain figures of arithmetical subtlety sent for the sake of amusement." Charles himself refers to his excursions with Alcuin "through the plains of arithmetical art," and Alcuin speaks in one of his poems of "studying the fair forms of numbers" with Charles. The *propositiones* consist in the main of very simple exercises, all solved by painfully rudimentary methods. Not one of them exhibits an apprehension on Alcuin's part of any mathematical idea or formula. Forty-five of the fifty-three propositions may, by courtesy, be styled exercises in reckoning. Each one is twofold in its structure, containing the *propositio* and its attached *solutio*. They are put in the style of a master towards his pupils, the proposition generally culminating in some such formula as "let him solve this who can" (*solvat qui potest*), or, "let him that understandeth say how we must divide," or simply, "let him who is able answer." The propositions themselves are various, but are confined to a few kinds of questions, all put in concrete form and sometimes jocosely. Occasionally there is no regard paid to the probability of the state of things pictured in the proposition. Thus a king is represented as gathering an army

in geometrical progression, one man in the first
town, two in the second, four in the third, eight in
the fourth, and so on through thirty towns.   The
total is 1,073,741,823 soldiers, an army whose
number might well amuse the imperial pupil.   Of
course Alcuin is entirely ignorant in this problem of
any formula for the sum of a geometrical progression, and so he proceeds to count it all out.   The
solutions are alarmingly infantile in their methods.
The numerals are Roman, and this adds enormously
to the slowness of working the examples.   The only
processes employed are the simplest operations of
addition, multiplication, and division, commonly
neglecting all "remainders" in division, and there
is rarely any use of subtraction.   Common fractions
of a very elementary sort are at times used, but no
fractional symbols are employed.   They are spoken
of as "the half," "the half of the half," "the third
part," "the sixth part," and "the eleventh part."
They are not treated as fractions, but as divisors.
"Aliquot parts" frequently figure in constructing the puzzles, and there are some examples
of finding areas of triangles, always isosceles,
and of quadrangular and "round" figures.   His
forty-second proposition is unique, in being clever.
There is a ladder with one hundred steps.   One
dove is on the first step, two on the second, three on
the third, and so on.   How many doves are on the
ladder?   On the first and ninety-ninth steps there
are accordingly one hundred doves, and so on the
second and ninety-eighth steps.   Proceeding thus

through the pairs of steps, we find forty-nine pairs of steps, each containing one hundred doves, with the fiftieth and hundredth steps omitted, which last contain jointly one hundred and fifty doves. The total is accordingly five thousand and fifty. In this example Alcuin unconsciously goes through the process which underlies arithmetical progression. Some of the propositions are properly algebraical, involving the simple equation in one unknown quantity, but of course he is not aware of this and works them out mechanically.

Not only are the methods of solution employed so crude, but no principle of arithmetic ever seems to dawn upon his mind. Cumbrous manipulation of particular problems is his only accomplishment. The character of most of the problems solved is depressing to think about. Of course they are concrete and meant to be witty. They are "*ad acuendos juvenes.*" They are "figures of arithmetical subtlety" meant to whet the wit of youth, but it is surely startling to read of a sty that holds 262,304 pigs, as one which some unknown *quidam* has constructed, starting with one sow and a litter of seven; — and all this invented to get an example in multiplication. Other examples are equally silly without being funny. Quadrangular houses are to be put into a triangular city so as to fill the triangle completely, or into a "round" city with a similar result, the answers being worked out in entire unconsciousness of the logical impossibility involved. Leaving the semi-arithmetical exercises,

we have a variety of trivial puzzles remaining.
After an ox has plowed all day, how many steps
does he take in the last furrow? The answer is,
"none, because the last furrow covers his tracks."
This would serve as well for the first or for any or
for all furrows. When a farmer goes plowing,
and has turned thrice at each end of his field, how
many furrows has he drawn? Alcuin says six, but
the Venerable Bede said seven, and the Venerable
Bede was right, if only the farmer starts in his
first furrow on a straight line from one end of the
field and finishes his last furrow. In another proposition Alcuin requests that three hundred pigs be
killed in three batches on successive days, an odd
number to be killed each day. But as three odd
numbers cannot add up an even sum, he has an
impregnably insoluble proposition. "*Ecce fabula!*"
he cries in glee, "here's a go! There is no solution. This fable is only to provoke boys." He
adds a scholium at the end to the effect that the
proposition will work in the same way if only
thirty pigs are taken.

Let not Alcuin's treatises be judged apart from
the environment of his times. The age, whose
intellect he addressed, thought as a child and spake
as a child, and to have presented anything else was
to present what it could not understand. It was to
invite certain failure in any attempt made in behalf
of learning. It was a necessary first stage in the
evolution of modern European culture that some
one should at some time teach the rudiments to

barbarous western Europe, and that Alcuin did this and recognized the limitations under which learning would be received, is not so much a proof of mediocrity as of his sagacity. He was not a writer of genius, nor of originality, nor of vast learning, but he was a man of great practical sense.

Nor should his properly didactic writings furnish the basis for a judgment as to the educational attainments of their author, except as exhibiting the substance of his formal instruction. If this is all we have, then the best that can be said for his teaching is that he gave western Europe imperfectly understood fragments of the wisdom of the ancients, and is more significant from the fact that he makes plain the intellectual darkness of the time than that he is introducing a learning that relieves it. Happily, there is another side to his educational activity which appears in many of his letters. They give us many a glimpse of his utter unselfishness, his purity and gentleness, his fidelity to the spiritual welfare of his pupils, and his never-ceasing personal anxiety that their lives and minds should be moulded by the spirit of Christ. Here is the true Alcuin, not the reviver of a decayed and fragmentary school learning, but the inspirer of Christian ideals, both as to studies and conduct, in an age when both seemed to be disappearing from the face of Europe.

Alcuin's eye followed his pupils in their later life and his hand of support or restraint was outstretched to them again and again. When one of

them, who was fond of high living and the company
of actors, was going to Italy, he cautioned him soberly
not only as to the care of his health in that climate,
but as to his general conduct. "My dearest son,"
he writes, "great is my longing for your health
and prosperity. I therefore desire to send you a
letter of exhortation in place of the spoken words
of paternal affection, beseeching you to keep God
before your eyes and in your remembrance with
entire devotion of mind and virtuous intention.
Let Christ be on your lips and in your heart. Act
not childishly and follow not boyish whims, but be
perfect in all uprightness and continence and moderation, that God may be glorified by your works,
and that the father who bore you may not be made
ashamed. Be temperate in food and drink, regarding rather your own welfare than any carnal
delight or the vain praise of men, which profiteth
not if your acts be displeasing to God. It is better to please God than to please actors, to look
after the poor than to go after buffoons. Let
your feastings be decorous, and those who feast
with you be religious. Be old in morals, though
young in years." Another letter written from
Tours in Alcuin's old age to the young princes still
at the palace, when Charles, their father, was away
in Italy, is both tender and playful in its affection.
It reads in part: "To my dearest sons in Christ
their father wisheth eternal welfare. I would write
you a great deal if only I had a dove or a raven
that would carry my letter on its faithful pinions.

Nevertheless, I have given this little sheet to the winds, that it may come to you by some favoring breeze, unless, perchance, the gentle zephyr change to an eastern blast. But arise, O south or north or any wind! and bear away this little parchment to bid you greeting and to announce our prosperity, and our great desire to see you well and whole, even as the father desires his sons to be. Oh, how happy was that day when amid our labors we played at the sports of letters! But now all is changed. The old man has been left to beget other sons, and weeps for his former children that are gone."

In his little book, *On The Virtues and Vices*, sent to Count Wido for his moral instruction, he commends to him the reading of the Scriptures in words of quiet serenity and deep spirituality. "In the reading of the Holy Scriptures," he writes, "lies the knowledge of true blessedness, for therein, as in a mirror, man may consider himself, what he is and whither he goes. He who would be always with God ought frequently to pray and frequently to read, for when we pray we are speaking with God, and when we read God is speaking to us." More than one letter of Alcuin's to wayward pupils has come to us. To one of them he writes in the following manner: "A mourning father sends greeting to his prodigal son. Why hast thou forgotten thy father who taught thee from infancy, imbued thee with the liberal disciplines, fashioned thy morals, and fortified them with the precepts of eternal life, to join thyself to the company of harlots, to the feastings of revellers, to the vanities of the proud? Art not thou that youth that was once a praise in the mouth of all, a delight to their eyes, and a pleasure to their ears? Alas! alas! now art thou a reproach in the mouth of all, the curse of their eyes and the detestation of their ears. What has so overturned thee but drunkenness and luxury? Who, O gracious boy, thou son and light of the Church, has persuaded thee to feed the swine and to eat of their husks? Arise, my son, arise, and return to thy father and say not once, but often, 'Father, I have sinned against heaven and in thy sight.'"

Such are a few out of many instances where Alcuin has left on record the secret of his power over the character of his pupils. He had been their master in things scholastic, but he was also their father in things spiritual.

CHAPTER VI

ALCUIN'S CHARACTER

IT is not surprising that conflicting judgments have been passed upon the character of Alcuin. He belonged to an age alien to our own both in the substance and manner of its intellectual life. He belonged, moreover, to an age wherein we see, with some confusion of vision, the disappearance of an old chaotic state of things and the emerging of a new social order, — one of those times in history when the cross-currents run so strongly that it often becomes hard to hold in view the true central drift of affairs. Besides this, it must be remembered that in his chief public activity he was a stranger in a strange land, and the characteristics of the raw, unformed Franks in their effect on the manifestation of his own traits among them, and through his behavior among them to us, must be taken into account. Additional elements which require to be appreciated are the Anglo-Saxon antecedents of Alcuin, his own personal traits so far as separable from his surroundings, the character of the teaching he received at York and of the masters who gave it, the actual sum of the learning of the time and the nature of his acquaintance with it, and the effect of his own

117

efforts upon his pupils and their successors. Thus, because of this complexity of elements and the additional embarrassment caused by the imperfection of our records, there have been almost as many opinions as writers about Alcuin. "Considering the period in which he lived, he may be regarded as a universal genius,"[1] is the judgment of one of his biographers. Another depicts him as "full of faith in the power and the destiny of man's intellect," and in fact quite a modern in his attitude.[2] The Abbé Laforêt in his sketch exceeds all bounds of moderation in eulogizing Alcuin's learning. "The erudition of Alcuin," he writes, "from whatever point it be viewed, embraced both the world of secular and of sacred learning. On one side he brings before us the most famous philosophers, historians and poets of Greece and Rome, and on the other exhibits a knowledge of the whole of ecclesiastical history and Christian doctrine."[3] Another, with more justice, rates him as "the most learned man of his age,"[4] but leaves the value of this opinion to be further determined by the character of the learning to which Alcuin had access. Less complimentary, as well as disappointing is the judgment which makes him merely "an estimable man, and a good administrator, but of no

---

[1] Lorenz, *Life of Alcuin*, London, 1837, p. 245.

[2] Monnier, *Alcuin et Charlemagne*, p. 357.

[3] Laforêt, *Alcuin Restaurateur des Sciences en Occident sous Charlemagne*, p. 245.

[4] *Histoire Littéraire de la France*, Vol. IV, p. 344.

original genius, and cast in a monastic mould." [1]
From these diverse estimates, whether eulogistic
or depreciatory, of Alcuin's scholarly qualities,
it is a relief to turn to such a well-balanced judgment as that which asserts that "Alcuin was rather
a man of learning and action than of genius and
contemplation, like Bede, but his power of organization and of teaching was great, and his services
to religion and literature in Europe, based indeed
on the foundation of Bede, were more widely extended, and in themselves inestimable." [2]

The same contrariety is discoverable in the estimates put on other phases of Alcuin's character.
Thus his humility seems to one ostentatious, and
to another genuine. His timidity becomes either
rank cowardice or wise prudence. His conservative distrust of anything outside the Roman tradition is interpreted both as a trait which "dwarfs
him almost to littleness," [3] and as the saving quality
of all his teaching. [4]

Underneath these diversities, due in part to the
point of view of the writers and in part to an attention bestowed on certain aspects of Alcuin's character to the obscuring of others, and thus leading to
casual error or even serious disproportion, there is

[1] Laurie, *Rise and Early Constitution of Universities*, p. 47.
[2] "Alcuin," by Bishop Stubbs, in the *Dictionary of Christian
Biography*.
[3] Mullinger, *Schools of Charles the Great*, p. 126.
[4] Laforêt, *Alcuin Restaurateur des Sciences en Occident sous
Charlemagne*, p. 247, note 2.

yet an agreement as to much that is essential.
After all, the original and proper personality of
Alcuin, as distinguished from any modified mani-
festations of his character under stress of circumstances, which at times obscured his real self, is
not very difficult to discover and portray. He was
a man of pure and unselfish character, thoroughly
penetrated by a deep and gentle piety joined to
strong moral earnestness. Inwrought with these
fundamental traits was his Anglo-Saxon sobriety
and fidelity, to which his training at the school in
York added habits of industry in study and vigorous
self-control in morals. The models which he consciously aspired to imitate were those characters
which had themselves been moulded on the strict
lines of Church orthodoxy. His intellectual ideals
were thus limited by ecclesiastical tradition, and
hence his supreme aim as a teacher was to master
and communicate the existing learning so far as
adopted by the Church, without any thought of crit-
icism upon it or adventurous speculation beyond it.
Fidelity to received truth and not discovery of new
truth was accordingly his one passion as a student.
Whatever cramping effect such a conservative attitude would have had on the development of a learning that had once been planted and needed growth,
this injurious effect was not visible in Alcuin's
introduction of studies into Frankland. Indeed,
it was rather a help than a hindrance to the cause
of education that only what was generally accepted
as settled should be taught at the first. Alcuin

was therefore the man for his time. The airy
speculations of the bright Irish scholars, "their
versatility in everything, with sure knowledge of
nothing," [1] as Theodulf contemptuously put it, and
their general tendency to question the body of
accepted tradition, would have unfitted them to be
introducers and inculcators of the rudiments of a
school learning upon which any hope of future
progress might securely depend.

It was also well that Alcuin joined to his considerable learning both unselfishness of purpose and
great tact. Though Charles assigned rich bene-
fices for his support, he remained a poor man to
the end of his life, using the means at his command
to further the cause of learning. Though in the
line of succession to the archbishopric of York, he
was indifferent to this as to all other ecclesiastical
advancement, content to be a simple deacon or
"humble Levite," as he so often styles himself.
His influence was thus more evidently the result
of his own personal qualities than of the accidents
of ecclesiastical station, and the example of self-
denial which he set to his scholars proclaimed
eloquently enough the excellence of learning over
the advantages of wealth and position. "It is
easy indeed to point out to you the path of wisdom," was his noble encouragement to them, "if
only ye love it for the sake of God, for knowledge,
for purity of heart, for understanding the truth,
yea, and for itself. Seek it not to gain the praise

[1] Migne, Vol. CV, 322.

of men, or the honors of this world, nor yet for
the deceitful pleasures of riches, for the more these
things are loved so much the farther do they cause
those who seek them to depart from the light of
truth and knowledge."[1] This is the spirit of his
best teaching, and in this, if in nothing else, he is
the finest soul of his age; nor has any age since
his time either outlived or lived up to his monition.

We must also credit him with a certain largeness
of view in spite of his circumscribed horizon. He
had some notion of the continuity of the intellectual
life of man, of the perils that be set the transmission of learning from age to age, and of the disgrace that attached to those who would allow those
noble arts to perish which the wisest of men among
the ancients had discovered. He saw clearly that
it was vitally important for education to pervade
the Church, wherein all hopes of learning were then
centred, and that it was also valuable as a civilizing
agent in the world. Bestowing his instruction in the
first instance on those who were to be churchmen,
he also taught clerks and laymen alike at York, at
Aachen and at Tours, not for hire, not for osten-
tation of his erudition, but without money and
without price, for the love of souls. Perceiving
that the precious treasure of knowledge was then
hidden in a few books, he made it his care to
transmit to future ages copies undisfigured by
slips of the pen or mistakes of the understanding.
Thus, in every way that lay within his power,

[1] *Grammatica*, Migne, CI, 850.

he endeavored to put the fortunes of learning for the times that should succeed him in a position of advantage, safeguarded by an abundance of truthfully transcribed books, interpreted by teachers of his own training, sheltered within the Church and defended by the civil power.

In view of such inestimable services, it becomes a matter of small concern to seek after his defects. They are visible enough, so far as important to an understanding of his place in education, in the limitations which define his ideals and achievements. Therefore, let the best he wrought be taken as reflecting Alcuin at his best, exhibiting, as in a fine likeness, the expression for which he most deserves to be remembered.

CHAPTER VII

RABANUS MAURUS AND ALCUIN'S OTHER PUPILS

AT the time of Alcuin's death, the chief posts of advantage for promoting the cause of education within the empire of Charles the Great were held by his pupils or friends. Theodulf was bishop of Orleans, the adviser of Charles in his later years, and of his successor, Lewis the Pious. His beloved Arno was archbishop of Salzburg, Riculf of Mayence, Rigbod of Treves, and Leidrad of Lyons; while the younger Eanbald, as archbishop of York, might be depended upon to foster sound learning in Britain. Adelhard, the princely cousin of Charles the Great, who had retired from court when a young man to enter the abbey of Corbie near Amiens, had become its abbat, and after the death of Alcuin founded the abbey of new Corbie in Saxony in 822, becoming its first abbat and remaining at the head of both monasteries until his death in 826. Angilbert ruled the abbey of St. Riquier. Sigulf became abbat of Ferrieres, one of the houses whose revenues had been assigned to Alcuin on his coming into Frankland. On the death of Sigulf in 821, Aldrich, who had studied at Tours, succeeded him as abbat of Ferrieres, and so continued until 829, when he became archbishop

of Sens. He also taught theology for a while in
the palace school, and was instrumental in reform-
ing the discipline of the abbey of St. Denis. He
died at Ferrieres in 836. Alcuin's favorite pupil,
Fridugis, by his desire succeeded him as head of
the monastery and school at Tours in 804, continuing there until his death in 834. His friend and
correspondent, St. Benedict, ruled the monastery
at Aniane in Languedoc. Others of his pupils
of lesser fame were scattered here and there in
various schools, while the greatest and almost the
latest of his disciples, young Rabanus Maurus, the
primus præceptor Germaniæ, was already teaching
in the school at Fulda, destined under his presi-
dency to become more famous than Tours itself.

"In that part of Germany which the eastern
Franks inhabit," writes Rudolph, the contemporary biographer of Rabanus, "there is a place
called Fulda from the name of a neighboring river.
It is situated in a great forest which in modern
times is called *Buchonia,* or Beechwood, by the
inhabitants of those parts. The holy martyr Boniface, who was sent as an ambassador from the
apostolic see into Germany and ordained bishop
of the church of Mayence, obtained this woodland,
inasmuch as it was secluded and far removed from
the goings and comings of men, from Carloman,
king of the Franks, and by authority of Pope
Zacharias founded a monastery there in the tenth
year before his martyrdom, being the seven hundred
and forty-fourth year after the birth of our Lord.

"Now the fifth abbat appointed to rule over the monastery after the blessed Boniface was Rabanus, who was also my preceptor, a man deeply religious and well instructed in Holy Scripture, whose whole study was given to meditation in the law of the Lord and to the teaching of truth, and moreover to exercising the greatest care over monastic discipline and the advancement of his scholars."

Rabanus was born in Mayence in 776. While yet a child he was sent to the abbey school of Fulda to be educated, and at once embraced the monastic life. The school had already attained great reputation. Its foundation had been laid by Boniface, the "apostle of Germany." Sturm, the first abbat, had visited the Italian abbeys in 747, in search of a pattern for his own, and on his return modeled the abbey and its school after Monte Cassino, the foremost of the Benedictine houses. Its second abbat was Baugulf, who ruled from 780 to 802, coincident with almost the whole time of Alcuin's activity in the palace school and at Tours. Being then one of the leading abbeys, it was directly affected by the educational revival instituted by Charles under Alcuin's guidance, and the copy of the great capitulary of 787 addressed to Baugulf is the only one that has been preserved to modern times. Rabanus pursued his youthful studies under him and his successor Ratgar, whose interest in his brilliant pupil was deep and constant.

Ratgar was soon attracted by the fame of Alcuin, and an old manuscript of Fulda records the fact that in the year 802 he sent "Rabanus along with Hatto to Tours unto Master Albinus, for the sake of learning the liberal arts." Rabanus was not unmindful of the kindness, and in some verses to Ratgar records his gratitude and laments his defective memory, but assures Ratgar that whatever his master taught him was all faithfully committed to writing. "It is thy goodness," he says, "that has enabled me to study books, but the poverty of my own mind stifles me. Wherefore, whatsoever my master taught me by word of mouth I committed entire to the leaves of books, lest my wandering wits should lose it."[1] As companions of his studies at Tours, Rabanus had Hatto, already mentioned, who succeeded him as abbat of Fulda, Haymo, later archbishop of Halberstadt, and Samuel, who became abbat of Lorsch. He never forgot his student days under Alcuin. In the preface of his encyclopedia, *On the Universe*, Rabanus recalls to Haymo the days spent at Tours "in the study of letters and meditation on the Scriptures, when we read together not only the sacred books and the expositions of the holy fathers thereon, but also those acute inquisitions of the 'prudent of this world' into the nature of things, recorded in their descriptions of the liberal arts and their other investigations."[2] Alcuin so highly esteemed his pupil that he bestowed on him, after his custom, the special surname Maurus, after St. Maur, the

[1] Poem to Ratgar (*Carm.* XIV), Migne, CXII, 1600.
[2] *De Universo*, Preface to Haymo, Migne, CXI, 11.

favorite pupil of St. Benedict. After a stay of
not more than a year at Tours, Rabanus returned
to Fulda, and was at once put in charge of the
abbey school by Ratgar, with Alcuin's full approval, as may be inferred from a short letter [1]
he wrote to Rabanus in the year 803, invoking a
blessing upon him and his scholars. But his
interest did not cease here, and a still later letter
shows that he and Rabanus kept up a close correspondence. [2]

In this letter Alcuin congratulates Rabanus on
his becoming devotion to "sacred wisdom" and

[1] Ep. 251 Jaffé; 187 Migne.

[2] Litterarum series tuarum lætificavit oculos meos. Ep. 290
Jaffé.

It is true this letter of Alcuin is not directed to Rabanus by
name, but it contains indications that it was sent to him. In the
salutation, Alcuin greets his " dearly beloved son and pet animal
(animali)." Rabanus means " a raven " (rabe), and the designation " pet animal " is in keeping with a humorous habit Alcuin
had of playing on the names of his pupils in his letters to them.
Moreover, the letter is addressed to one who is commended for
his excellence in studies, and abounds in exhortations regarding
the teaching of youth who are then subject to him. Still more
conclusive is the fact that the recipient of the letter is said to have
been " a fellow-disciple of Samuel," whom Rabanus himself in
one of his poems styles the special sodalis of his earlier days.
" My beloved brother," he says in his twenty-second poem, " it
was once my joy to have thee as my companion among the other
students. Remember me now as I remember you, and let your
heart retain and your conduct exhibit that which once our
master Albinus taught us." (Migne, CXII, 1604.)

Duemmler argues from the mention of Samuel, without observ-
ing the other considerations, that the letter was sent to Rabanus
(Monumenta Alcuiniana, p. 876, note). Froben inclines to the
same view (Migne, vol. C, 459, note on " Samuelis ").

his "love of learning." In response to a previous request that Alcuin should write an account of his own conduct and habits so that he might imitate them, his master expresses surprise that he should need these. "It seems a marvel," he writes, "for you to ask me to describe my conduct, since you were with me day and night, nor was anything that I did ever concealed from you." He then reminds him that he would do far better to imitate the examples of the holy men whose lives are recorded in Scripture, and above all exhorts him "to seek after Christ as foretold by the prophets and set forth in the gospel." "And when you find him," he continues, "do not let him go, but bring him into the house of your heart and keep him as the master of your life." He also instructs him to be careful of his office as a teacher, that the gift of intelligence in him may be increased; "for 'unto him that hath shall be given,' that is, to him that hath a desire of teaching shall be added the discernment of understanding." His pupils are exhorted "to learn in their youth, that they may be able to teach when they are old."

Samuel helped Rabanus in his school work, and there were other assistants. The library of the abbey was greatly enriched, possibly drawing some of its books from Tours.[1] In a poem to Gerhoch, the librarian, whom Rabanus fancifully styles his "clavipotens frater," or "brother with the power of

[1] *Alcuin*, Ep. 290 Jaffé. Rabanus asked for books from Alcuin.

the keys," he describes the extent of the library.
"What can I say," he exclaims, "in the high praise
of books, — the books which you, dear brother,
keep beneath your key? There is to be found
whatsoever the wisdom of the world has published
in its various ages." The exaggerations of verse
need not cause us to doubt that the library was
ample and one of the completest for its time. A
large part of it could doubtless be reconstructed by
title out of the list of writers quoted by Rabanus
in his own works. The importance he attached to
it is also another indication that he was following
hard after the example Alcuin had set at Tours in
using the library as an indispensable aid to the
school. He had many pupils, and some of them
became famous. Such were Walafrid Strabo,
Servatus Lupus, Rudolph, his biographer, and
Otfried of Weissenburg. It is probable that the
whole number of his scholars largely exceeded
Alcuin's, for there are very few names of men
eminent in education during the next age which
may not be traced back to Fulda or its twenty-
two affiliated lesser schools. Meanwhile Eigil, the
fourth abbat, passed away, and Rabanus succeeded
him in 822. He then gave over the charge of teaching the liberal arts to others, reserving to himself
the interpretation of Scripture. His career as abbat
was famous. Under his rule the monastery at Fulda
rapidly increased its endowments, and the number
of its students and affiliated schools. Its fame for
learning and sanctity spread through all of Frank-

land as well as Germany, and extended even to
Italy. Rabanus became the adviser of kings and
princes, and even of the pope, and was looked up
to with special veneration as being the one on
whom the mantle of Alcuin had fallen.

After ruling the abbey for twenty years, he
retired in 842. The brethren urgently sought to
recall him. But as he refused, they elected Hatto
in his place. Rabanus then went into retirement
at Petersberg near by, and devoted his attention
to meditation and writing. In 847 he was made
archbishop of Mayence, and died in the year 856,
in a neighboring village on the banks of the Rhine,
whence his body was taken back to Mayence for
burial.

He was not only Alcuin's greatest pupil, but a
much greater man than his master. He was made
in a larger mould. While a conservative son of the
Church, he endeavored to develop rather than to
confine the ecclesiastical tradition in education,
and is entirely lacking in that timorous shrinking
from everything outside the traditional limits which
so cramped Alcuin's intellectual exercises. The
heathen weapon of dialectics, which had been looked
on as a dangerous two-edged sword, he grasped
without hesitation to wield for the truth. He
recalled grammar from being a barren study of
words and letters and syllables, and connected it
again with the study of literature. Instead of treating astronomy as merely a ready-reckoning machine
for working out the church calendar, he urged its

study as a lofty intellectual exercise. And so with the other disciplines. Though unable to disengage himself from most of the prevalent errors of his time, he must be credited with improving on Alcuin's treatment of the liberal arts to a very marked degree. The whole volume of secular learning expanded under his teaching and yet without prejudice to the study of Scripture. He also contributed distinctly to the general advance of thought which ended in bringing in scholasticism. He boldly insisted on applying the processes of reason to systematizing the facts of religion, and in this occupies a middle position between the irresponsible speculative spirit of Erigena and the uncritical crudeness of tradition.

The whole temper of his mind was more open and courageous than Alcuin's. When he came to deal with natural events, he did not childishly seek to ascribe them to occult causes, but referred them to the order of nature established by the Creator; and so, when a superstitious mob in his time sought to "bring help to the waning moon" by their cries and shouts, with the beating of drums and sounding of horns, he rebuked them, bidding them remember that the regular changes and even the portents in the skies were all the work of a wise Creator who was able to manage the world he had made. There was also in him, as might have been expected, marked generosity and sympathy. He was more than once reproved for being over-liberal to the poor, and in the time of famine exerted himself unsparingly to relieve the distress. The only instance of unjust severity to another that attaches to his name was the flogging of the monk Gotteschalk by his order for heretical teaching touching the doctrine of predestination. But, setting this aside, Rabanus, though a strict disciplinarian, was likewise a humane man through all his life. He was also prudent, for in the midst of bloody dissensions and plots that thickened around the successors of Charles the Great, and the violent internal strife which rent his own monastery before he became abbat, he so deported himself as to preserve the regard of every faction. Taken as a whole, the personality of Rabanus charms us by its independence and vigor, tempered, as it was, by humanity, good sense, and a loyal respect for the Church he served.

On the educational side, however, his activity as a teacher and a writer chiefly call for notice, and both of these are seen to the best advantage in his important educational works, which deserve separate and somewhat detailed examination.

His works, which have come to us substantially entire, are indeed voluminous, being collectively at least three times greater in extent than those of his teacher Alcuin, and ominously suggest the monumental vastness of the scholastic writings yet to come. Most of his writings, perhaps seven-eighths in all, are theological, being devoted chiefly to a series of elaborate commentaries, expositions, and "narrations" on thirty-three books of the Old and New

Testament, including a complete explanation, literal, allegorical, and mystical, of the Pentateuch and nearly all the historical books of the Old Testament, together with Proverbs, Jeremiah and Ezekiel, as well as the Gospel of Matthew and all the epistles of St. Paul. In all this he was only following after the ideal that was ever before him of acquainting himself and others with the whole plenitude of Scripture. For "in the knowledge of Holy Scripture," as he writes in his book *On the Instruction of the Clergy*, "is the foundation, the establishment and the perfecting of wisdom."[1] Herein is contained the wisdom that flows from the eternal and unchangeable Wisdom, even from the mouth of the Most High himself. It is "first-born before all other creatures." The unfailing light that burns within the Scriptures "streams forth over all the world as though let out from a lantern." By that light he studied, devoting his long life to a whole-souled and untiring attempt to set forth their supreme excellency.

But in addition to his theological writings, Rabanus composed several treatises which bear in whole or in part on education. These are the works, *On the Instruction of the Clergy*, *On Reckoning*, *An Excerpt on the Grammatical Art of Priscian*, *On the Universe* (which may equally well be entitled *On Everything*), a short *Latin-Tudesque Glossary*, and a tract *On the Origin of Languages*. Perhaps to these should be added his short *Treatise*

[1] *De Clericorum Institutione*, III, cap. 2.

on the Soul, which, like Alcuin's on the same subject, is based on Augustine.

His work *On the Instruction of the Clergy*[1] was written in the year 819 in response to urgent requests from the monks of Fulda and others that he should compose a compendium of the things most necessary for the clergy to know. It is divided into three books. The first deals with the organization of the Church, its orders of clergy, its vestments and sacraments. The second describes the round of ecclesiastical duties, the feasts and fasts of the year, and parts of the church service, including also some notice of the books of Scripture, the orthodox creed and the various opposing heresies. The third book, as Rabanus states, "teaches how all that is written in the sacred books is to be searched and studied, as well as those things in the arts and studies of the heathen which are useful for an ecclesiastic to inquire into."[2]

It is this third book which has educational interest, for, although primarily intended as a manual for the education of clergy, it contains much that relates to secular learning. The book opens with the proposition that any one who would fulfil the sacred clerical duties ought to be a man of "plenitude of knowledge, rectitude of life and perfection of erudition." Rabanus goes on to define this more fully by saying, "Such an one should not be allowed

[1] *De Clericorum Institutione* in Migne's *Patrologia Latina,* CVII, 293-419.

[2] *De Clericorum Institutione,* Præfatio.

to be ignorant of any of those things wherein it will be his duty to instruct both himself and those who are subject to him, that is, of the Holy Scriptures, of the clear truth of history, of the modes of figurative speech, of the signification of mystical things, of the utility of all the disciplines, of uprightness of life and probity of morals, of elegance in the delivery of discourses, of wisdom in the setting forth of doctrines and of the different remedies suited to the variety of spiritual diseases."[1] His educated man is, therefore, to be conversant with Scripture, with history, with an understanding of the figures of speech and the mystical sense of things, and of all the useful knowledge in the different liberal disciplines. Besides this, he is to be a man of probity in life and especially accomplished in rhetoric and dialectics. "One who does not know these things is not only unable to be useful to others, but even to himself. Therefore it is needful that the future ruler of a people, while he has leisure, should prepare in advance the weapons whereby he may bravely conquer the enemy and defend the flock committed to him. For it is a base thing that one who has been appointed a pastor of souls should only begin to desire to learn at the time when he ought to be ready to teach, and it is a perilous thing for any one to take up the burden of a ruler if he cannot ably support that burden by the strength of his own wisdom." And then comes one of those

[1] *De Clericorum Institutione*, I, 1.

golden sentences wherein we hear Rabanus at his
best. "Let no one dare to teach any art, unless
he has first learned it by prolonged study." [1] The
imperative tone was needed, for he was waging
relentless war against the promotion of ignorant
clergy to posts of honor. "There are some," he
says, " who within the Church itself seek promotion
solely from ambition. As the Scripture attests, it
is they who covet the first salutations in the market-
place, the chief places at feasts, and the chief seats
in the synagogues. . . . They are the ignorant
shepherds who are reproved by the prophet Isaiah,
saying, 'These are shepherds that cannot understand.' By reason of their ignorance, those who
follow them stumble, and hence in the gospel
Christ the Truth saith, 'If the blind lead the blind,
they shall both fall into the ditch.'" By such
scriptural exhortation and illustration Rabanus
develops the opening chapter of the third book,
and prepares the way for setting forth the education needed for the elevation of the clergy.

He then proceeds in the second chapter to explain
that knowledge of Holy Scripture is both the beginning and the completion of wisdom, because Scripture is the highest utterance of God himself, the
eternal Wisdom. Whatever truth there may be
elsewhere, whether in the Church or out of it, has
its source, it is true, in the same eternal Wisdom
from which the Scriptures come. But as Scripture

[1] Nulla ars doceri præsumatur, nisi prius intenta meditatione
discatur. I, 1.

is the transcendent and highest utterance of the
Divine Wisdom, so is it superior to the wisdom
found in the Church or in the world outside. Yet as
all truth has one source he goes on to say: "Whatever truth there may be anywhere is to be known as
truth by bringing it to a test of truth, and whatever good there is anywhere is discovered to be
good by a standard of goodness. Nor are the true
and wise things which are to be found in the books
of the 'prudent of this world' to be attributed to
any other source than truth and wisdom itself,
because these truths were not constructed originally
by those in whose writings they are found, but
were truths existing from eternity which they
merely discovered. For Truth and Wisdom, the
teacher and enlightener of all, granted them the
power to search them out. Therefore, all the useful knowledge that lies in the books of the heathen,
and the salutary truths of Scripture as well, are to
be used for one purpose and referred to one end,
that is, the perfect knowledge of truth and the
highest excellence of wisdom." This is Augustine
revived in his most generous mood, speaking by the
voice of Rabanus. The cramping and shrinking
of Alcuin's spirit is no longer here, and in such a
passage as this Rabanus when compared with him
seems a giant. The book then goes on to explain
the spirit and method of studying the Scriptures,
closely following the treatise of Augustine *On
Christian Doctrine.*[1]

[1] *De Clericorum Institutione*, III, cap. 15, at the end.

Beginning at the sixteenth chapter, eleven successive chapters are devoted to secular learning, a separate one being assigned to each of the seven liberal
arts. Rabanus first distinguishes between the fun-
damentally true things of ancient secular learning
and the false inventions which were attached to it.
Such were all magic arts, the worship of idols, the
taking of omens, astrological calculations, and the
other varieties of "pernicious superstition." On
the other hand the body of human learning, which
is so needful for our life here below, is by no
means to be despised by a Christian. Nay, he
insists, it should be "studied and held firmly in
mind," and whoso does this will understand, the
more he studies, that the whole of truth taken as
one redounds to the "honor and love of one God."[1]
His following account of the liberal arts separately
is of distinct interest. Grammar he defines as
"the science of interpreting the poets and historians, and the art of correct writing and speaking. It is the foundation of the liberal arts."
Alcuin had confined grammar to the explanation
of how to write and speak correctly. Rabanus
adds to this narrow formal side the literary side,
which was included in the broader definition of the
Roman grammarians, and thereby rescues it from
the barrenness to which it had been reduced by the
treatment of Alcuin. However, he extols the
Christian against the classical poets, and cites

[1] Ad unius Dei laudem atque dilectionem cuncta convertere.
III, cap. 17.

Juvencus, Sedulius, Arator, Alcimus, Clement, Paulinus, and Fortunatus[1] as "writers of famous books." He allows with restriction the reading of classical poets, mainly for the sake of their "flowers of eloquence." "And so when we read the heathen poets, and the books of secular wisdom come into our hands," he writes by way of general conclusion, "let us turn to our own instruction whatever we find useful in them; but if there be anything superfluous concerning idols or love or the care of secular things," all such passages are to be passed by or expunged.

The chapter on rhetoric contains little of special note, but the next one on dialectics is important. "Dialectics," according to his definition, "is the rational discipline concerned with definitions and explanations, and able even to separate truth from falsehood." Such an utterance is in marked contrast with Alcuin, who would never have countenanced so bold and sweeping an assertion of the sufficiency of dialectics as a means of discerning between truth and error; but Rabanus waxes very bold and asserts further that "this is accordingly the discipline of disciplines. It teaches us how to teach and how to learn. In this Reason reveals herself, and shows clearly what she is, what she means and what she perceives. This discipline alone knows how to know, and is both willing and able to make others know. For when we

[1] It is interesting to notice that all these poets are in Alcuin's list of the books at York. See pages 34 and 35.

reason with it, we learn what we are and whence we are. We understand the difference between a good-doer and a good deed, between a creator and a creature. We investigate truth; we fasten on error. By this we reason and discern between what follows and what does not follow; what is inconsistent, what is true, and what is probable, as well as what is thoroughly false."

While Rabanus cannot be credited, as some have supposed, with an important advance on Boethius and with consciously opening up the dialectical activity of the early Middle Ages, it is yet true that his enthusiastic commendation of dialectics was influential in preparing the way for the reign of logic later.[1] Of course such a weapon as Rabanus defined dialectics to be, must have eminent value for the Church. "Wherefore," he says, "the clergy ought to know this most noble art and to have its laws constantly before them in meditation, that they may be able to penetrate with subtlety into the craftiness of the heretics, and confute their opinions by the magical conclusions of syllogisms." His speculative contemporary, Scotus Erigena, could have asked little more. Yet Rabanus guards himself by distinguishing between what he calls sophisms and truths. "There are true modes," he says, "of connecting not only true but even false

---

[1] So aüsserte die Schule welche Hrabanus bekanntlich in Fulda eingerichtet hatte . . . auch auf den Betrieb der Logik einen höchst günstigen Einfluss. — Prantl, *Geschichte der Logik*, II, 40.

opinions. Now, these true modes of connection may be learned in the schools which are outside the Church, but the truth of opinions is to be studied in the holy books of the Church." The forms of logic may be learned outside, but the substance of truth necessary for arriving at a sound conclusion can be learned only in books of the Church. And here, after all, is where his use of dialectics differs from that of Erigena. Rabanus would never have approved using Plato and Martianus Capella for substance of doctrine equal in value with Scripture, as Erigena did. And he was consistent, for after once asserting that the Scriptures are the highest form of truth and that other truths are to be interpreted in their light, the material for his reasoning was unchangeably defined and estimated in advance.

After thus treating grammar, rhetoric, and dialectics, he proceeds to describe the four remaining arts, which he includes, following a common custom, under the general name of mathematics. The first of the four is arithmetic, "the study of numerical quantity," pure and simple. It is, as he shows, the fundamental "mathematical discipline," without knowledge of which neither music, nor geometry, nor astronomy can be pursued. A Christian is not to despise this secular study, for does not Josephus, that most learned Jew, relate how Abraham was the first to deliver both the arithmetical and astronomical art to the Egyptians? The seed of this knowledge, which the father of the faithful sowed among them, they cultivated and also developed therefrom the other disciplines. Then, too, the Church fathers strongly commend the study of arithmetic, inasmuch as it abstracts the mind from carnal desires by leading it to abstract meditation. Scripture, too, commends the study in many places. God himself made the world "by measure and weight and number," as we read in the Book of Wisdom. Nay, more: "the very hairs of our head are numbered," as the gospel explicitly asserts. Then there are the writings of Plato, "of great authority," though less than Scripture, which represent to us the Creator building the universe according to numerical harmonies and proportions. Another consideration is to be found in the mystical significance of particular numbers mentioned in Scripture. "Thus," says Rabanus, "six is a perfect number, for did not God make the world in six days?" And yet he audaciously observes: "We are not to say that the number six is perfect because God accomplished his work of creation in six days, but that he accomplished the work in six days because six is a perfect number. Nay, even if his work had not been finished in six days, yet would the number still be a perfect one." Now, the Bible is really a sealed book to many because of their ignorance of arithmetic. "Wherefore," he writes, "it is needful, if any one would arrive at the knowledge of Holy Scripture, that he should study this art intently, so that when he has learned it he may the easier understand the mystical numbers in the sacred books." Alcuin would have commended heartily this exposition of arithmetic in general. Yet in two respects it departs from Alcuin, for Plato is quoted as "of great authority," though with some reserve, and a "perfect number" is represented as something regulative of the activity of God himself. Thus already in the barren field of arithmetic, as well as in dialectics, the shoots of speculation were beginning to spring up.

The account of geometry indicates that Rabanus had been reading one of Erigena's favorite books, the Latin translation by Chalcidius of the *Timæus* of Plato. "The philosophers," he says, "testify in their writings that Jupiter geometrizes." He prudently remarks that, "if this saying be applied wisely to God, the omnipotent Creator, it may perhaps be congruent with truth; for geometry, if we may be allowed to say so, has a holy divinity of its own, inasmuch as it imposes its various forms and models on creation, and maintains it in existence up to the present day." The courses of the stars and the "fixed linear" (*statutis lineis*) constitution of bodies in motion or at rest are cited as examples of the *sancta divinitas* of geometry. Its origin as an art is referred to the Egyptians, and Varro, "the most learned of the Latins," is cited to prove that geometry began with mensuration. A consideration which makes it acceptable to a Christian is, that it was used in building the tabernacle and the temple, in constructing which there was evident need "of the measurement of the line, the circle, the sphere, the hemisphere, and also of the

quadrangle." Lastly, "an acquaintance with all
geometrical figures is of help towards spiritual
discernment."

Music is defined as "the discipline which treats
of the numbers which pertain to it, that is, of those
which occur in sounds." "One sound," for example, "is the double, the treble, or the quadruple of
another." Music is so useful that without it the
church service cannot be fully performed, inasmuch
as not only pleasant modulation in singing but
proper pronunciation in reading call for musical
skill. It is also noble as well as useful. For
"the heaven and the earth and all that are in them
are ruled by harmony, Pythagoras testifying that
the world was created according to the harmonies
of music, and is governed by the same." Pythagoras, however, is not the only authority. The art
of music is blended with the Christian religion,
and ignorance of music is an impediment to faith.
No heed is to be paid to the heathen superstitions
which make the Muses daughters of Jove. The
learned Varro, a heathen himself, has refuted this
notion, showing that Jove was not the father of the
Muses. But whether Varro's opinion be true or
not makes little difference, "for we ought not to
avoid music, the art of the Muses, because of profane superstitions, so long as it is possible to extract
from it useful help for understanding Holy
Scripture." The folly of such a course would be
as great as a refusal to learn letters because the
heathen said Mercury was the god of letters, or to

refuse to practice justice and virtue because they
dedicated temples to Justice and Virtue. " On the
contrary," says Rabanus, echoing Augustine, "let
every good and true Christian know that all truth,
wherever he finds it, belongs to his Lord."

The exposition of astronomy, which next follows,
is lighted up with an enthusiasm almost as great
as appears in the account of dialectics. His opening statement is impressive. " If we pursue this
study with chastened and moderate spirit, it will,
as the ancients say, fill our thoughts with deep and
reverent love. How great a thing it is to approach in
spirit to the heavens, — to explore all their supernal
mechanism by rational investigation, and by lofty
intellectual insight to observe anywhere and everywhere the veiled secrets of their vast greatness!"
How feeble and poverty-stricken, in the light of
such a conception as this, is the interminable astronomical correspondence of Alcuin, which makes
of astronomy a cumbrous machine for calculating
the church feasts! Not that Rabanus refuses the
determination of the church calendar a place in
astronomy. On the contrary, he expressly includes
it therein. But astronomy is far more to him. It
is the study of the " law of the stars, which know
not either how to move or stop other wise than as
the Creator has ordained."

The seven arts have now passed in review.
"Here," he says, "are the seven liberal arts of
the philosophers." The " seven liberal arts"! It
is apparently the first instance in history of the

use of the term.   Christianity has at last succeeded after centuries in converting the *artes
liberales* of the ancients into the *septem artes liberales*.   The change of feeling from antagonism to
toleration, and then into friendly regard, slowly
outworking in Western Christendom from the time
of Augustine and Cassiodorus onward, ends with
the adoption of the liberal arts and the concurrent
prefixing of a Christian name to them.   So in
closing his account Rabanus commends them in
general as "useful for all Christians."   He goes
even farther, and adds that "anything the philosophers have written that is true and agreeable to
faith, especially the Platonic philosophers" (he
was not always quite ready to say Plato) "is not to
be viewed with alarm, but to be taken from them
for our own use."   By way of further enforcement,
he repeats what Augustine had said about taking
the gold and the silver of the Egyptians and avoiding their superstitions and idolatry.   As a final
and supreme caution, he reminds those who have
been instructed in the liberal arts to approach the
higher study of the Scriptures ever remembering
the apostolic watchword, *Scientia inflat, charitas
ædificat*" ("knowledge puffeth up, but love build-
eth up").

The rest of the work is devoted to miscellaneous
instruction on the art of speaking wisely and eloquently, with special reference to preaching.   His
remarks in the thirtieth chapter on the need of
using language easily comprehended when speaking

to the people "might well have been inscribed in letters of gold on every pulpit from his own to the present day." [1] They might equally well be inscribed on every teacher's desk. "Although a good teacher," he says, "ought to be so careful in his teaching that he will not consider an obscure or ambiguous word to be good Latin, still, while avoiding ambiguities and obscurities, let him speak after the fashion of the people, and not as the educated but as the uneducated speak. For of what value is that excellence of expression which the intellect of the hearer does not follow and which they do not understand to whom we are speaking in order that they may understand? Therefore, let him who teaches avoid all words that do not teach. [2] So then, if he can find other excellent words which will be understood, let him choose such; but if he cannot, either because there are no such words or because they do not occur to him at the time, let him use words that are less excellent, provided only the thing itself be taught and learned excellently." His reasons are no less sensible than his injunctions. "We must insist on being understood," [3] he says, "not only when we converse with one or a few persons, but much more when we speak in public, for in conversation every one has an opportunity to question us, but where all sit in silence listening

[1] Mullinger, *Schools of Charles the Great*, p. 145.

[2] Qui ergo docet, vitabit verba omnia quæ non docent. III, cap. 30.

[3] Ut intelligamur instandum est. III, cap. 30.

to one speaker, it is neither right nor decent to hold any auditor responsible for what he has not understood. For this reason he who speaks ought to make it his care to help him who silently listens. Now, an audience that is anxious to learn is apt to show by its own behavior whether it really understands or not. Until it does understand we should keep presenting the point at issue in various ways. Those who teach only what they have prepared and committed word by word to memory have not the power to accomplish this. Then when it is clear that the point is understood, continue the discourse and pass to the other points, for as he who makes clear what we wish to know is an acceptable teacher, so he becomes burdensome when inculcating what we already know." [1]

There is a statement in Trithemius, [2] a late biographer of Rabanus, that he wrote while a youth *Præparamenta*, or hand-books of the seven liberal arts "in many volumes." In the writings which have come to us, however, there are only two treatises on separate arts, and it is not certain that they are part of the *Præparamenta* mentioned by Trithemius. However, as treatises on two of the arts, they may be noticed here. One is entitled *An Excerpt on the Grammatical Art of Priscian*. It consists of extracts from the grammar of Priscian copied bodily with-

[1] Sicut enim gratus est qui agnoscenda enubilat, sic onerosus, qui cognita inculcat. III, cap. 30.

[2] Migne, *Patrologia Latina*, CVII, 103.

out indication of any authorship on the part of Rabanus, apart from a short poem added at the end. The other treatise is entitled *On Reckoning (Computus)*, and consists of ninety-six short chapters. It is the work of Rabanus, and was written in the year 820. Like some of Alcuin's writings, it is cast in the form of a dialogue between a master and his pupil. Augustine, Boethius, and Isidore are quoted in it, but Bede is the author most used in its preparation. The first eight chapters deal with the importance of numbers, the definition of the term " number " itself, the different kinds of numbers, treated grammatically rather than mathematically, — numbers being defined as cardinal, ordinal, adverbial, distributive, multiple, and " denuntiative." Then follow the two different reckonings, by letters and on the fingers. Notation is given both according to the Greek and the Roman numeral letters while the finger-reckoning described is one of the curiosities in educational history. The method of counting with the fingers is explained as follows: On the left hand there are three fingers, the little finger (*auricularis*), the fourth finger (*medicus*), and the third finger (*impudicus*). Accordingly the digits from one to nine can be counted by beginning with bending the little finger toward the palm, and so proceeding to make other number-gestures in sequence with the three fingers. Besides the three fingers mentioned, there are the index finger and the thumb, and by various flexions of these the tens are indicated from ten to ninety, so that with the left hand alone every number short of one hundred could be counted. Then there is the right hand, where the counting begins with the thumb and the index finger, and then proceeds to the three other fingers, — just the reverse of the method used in counting on the left hand. The right-hand thumb and finger are used by various flexions to indicate the hundreds from one hundred to nine hundred, and the three other fingers on the right hand are used similarly to indicate the thousands from one thousand to nine thousand. Thus, if the two hands be spread out, palms down, units will be reckoned from the left on the little finger, the fourth finger, and the third finger of the left hand; tens will be reckoned on the index finger and thumb of the left hand; hundreds on the thumb and index finger of the right hand; thousands on the other three fingers of the right hand. Accordingly, the two hands taken together could be used to count up to any number short of ten thousand. This notation by finger flexion was extended still further by placing the left hand in various ways on different parts of the body, and so counting by tens of thousands, from ten thousand to ninety thousand; and in the same way the right hand when placed opposite corresponding parts of the body enabled counting to be done by the hundred-thousand, from one hundred thousand up to nine hundred thousand. An example or two of this barbarous method may be given. "When you say one," observes the master to his pupil, "bend the little finger on the left hand slightly inward and place it in the palm." "When you say ten, put the tip of the index finger against the middle of the thumb." Of course, eleven would be counted by doing both of these at once or in succession. In the same way a hundred is indicated on the right hand by putting the tip of the index finger against the middle of the thumb, just as ten was counted on the left hand. A thousand is indicated with the little finger of the right hand as one was indicated with the little finger of the left hand. Any number short of ten thousand could therefore be counted by the two hands without reference to the other parts of the body. For numbers from ten thousand upwards, a different method is used, as mentioned above. Ten thousand is indicated by placing the left hand flat on the breast, but with the fingers pointing upwards; and twenty thousand, with the same hand spread out flat across the chest; sixty thousand, with the same hand flat against the left thigh. The hundred-thousands are indicated in a similar manner with the right hand. Consequently, by a series of gestures any number short of a million may be indicated. The two hands clasped together in front, with the fingers intertwined, is the gesture for a million, which is the highest number of this digital reckoning. That such a system of gesture-numbers should have been deemed worthy of record and explanation by Rabanus for the benefit of the monks at Fulda is sad evidence of the crass ignorance that was prevalent. Counting on the fingers, the mode of reckoning in vogue among the lowest savages, awkward, cumbrous, devoid of any but the rudest intellectual quality, has often been characteristic of tribes which were never able to emerge from their barbarism. Whenever, therefore, we are tempted to look with contempt at the childishness of the best men of the early Middle Ages in their attempts to humanize and christianize the Saxon or the Frank, let the character of the material on which they were working be duly considered, and then their childishness is seen to be wisdom, because they essayed to do only what could be done in the circumstances. Or, as Rabanus might have put it himself, "They taught in the words that teach, not in those which do not teach."

The rest of his book on reckoning deals with the Roman divisions of weights, namely, the pound (*libra*), containing twelve ounces (*unciæ*), each ounce containing twenty-four scruples (*scripuli*), and each scruple in turn containing six *siliquæ*. He remarks that these names for weights may be applied not only to the varieties of money, but to divisions of time as well. He is in need of something to serve the purpose of fractions, and yet, like Alcuin, has no notion of what a fraction is. It is interesting to notice, however, that the sub-divisions of weights and measures are made on the scale of six or twelve, that is, are duodecimal, whereas the notation he described for integers was decimal. The divisions of time which occupy several chapters are odd enough. The smallest element of time is called the "atom." There are said to be three hundred seventy-six atoms in one "*ostentum*," which corresponds with our minute. The *ostentum* in turn is the sixtieth part of the hour, and one and one-half hours are called a "moment." The word "minute" occurs in Rabanus, but it means the tenth part of an hour, and the "point" is a quarter of an hour. Furthermore, "the hour is the twelfth part of a day," he continues, "for our Lord asserts this, saying, 'Are there not twelve hours in the day?'" The rest of the book is devoted to the parts of the year, the calendar in general, the phenomena of the sun, moon and planets, with the method of calculating Easter, including a singular method of calculating the lunar epact on the joints of the hand and closing remarks on the ages of the world's history. The *Computus* contains no examples in arithmetic, so that it is impossible to compare it intelligently with Alcuin's arithmetical propositions. It is to be regarded not as a formal treatise on arithmetic, but as a handbook of reckoning, including numbers, weights, and measures, the divisions of time, and so much astronomy as related to the general appearance of the sky, and the calculation of the church calendar.

In connection with his writings on the liberal arts it will be appropriate to notice the *Latin-Tudesque Glossary* attributed to him. It professes to be written down by his pupil, Walafrid Strabo, presumably from dictation. It contains less than two hundred Latin words, some of which are defined in Latin and others are given with their Tudesque equivalents. They are the names of the parts of the human body, and at the end are added the names of the months and the winds, in both languages. It is interesting as showing the incipient recognition of the vulgar languages on the part of the learned, and more especially the interest felt by Rabanus in the early German tongue. Even in Alcuin's time Latin was being pronounced in a barbarized fashion, which pointed to its coming fate. Rabanus had exhorted those who were to preach to speak so that the people could understand, and not to insist on learned propriety of expression. In this glossary he goes a step farther, and compiles a short list of words in frequent use in Latin with their vulgar Tudesque equivalents. Many of them have the lineaments of modern German. Thus the Latin *os* (mouth) is the Tudesque *mund;* the Latin *jecur* (liver) is *lebera*. For the Latin *pes* (foot) we have an approximation to the German *fuss* in the Tudesque *phuoz*.[1]

Rabanus is also credited with a short tract *On the Origin of Languages*.[2] Some of it is taken from Jerome. It contains, with comments, a Hebrew, a Greek and a Latin alphabet, with the sound of each letter indicated in Roman letters. Omega in Greek, for example, is called "*o longa.*" Then comes a

[1] Migne, CXII, 1575.
[2] *De Inventione Linguarum*, Migne, CXII, 1580.

supposed Scythian alphabet, which is briefly described and attributed to Jerome. Rabanus does not seem to be very sure that he understands it, for he says naively to his readers: "If we have committed any mistakes in this alphabet or any faults in the others, do you correct them." Then comes the alphabet used by the Marcomanni, "whom we call the Northmen, and from whom the tribes who speak the Tudesque language are descended." Following this are abbreviations for Roman proper names and the so-called *Notœ Cœsaris*, or "Marks of Cæsar," that is, combinations of dots used instead of vowels in Roman inscriptions. Last of all are some monograms of Scriptural names. As an essay in philology, there is, of course, nothing to be said about it. At best, it may pass for a hand-book of alphabets, useful for scribes, though probably not for general instruction in schools.

Passing by his treatise *On the Soul*,[1] which has only indirect educational bearings, there remains for consideration his encyclopedia of all knowledge, entitled *On the Universe*.[2] It was written about the year 844, after he had retired from the abbey of Fulda and gone into retreat at Petersberg. For the composition of such a work he naturally resorted to the huge *Etymologies* of Isidore of Seville, who had given the Middle Ages its first encyclopedia in twenty elaborate books. Following the example of Isidore, who had plundered the classical writers

---

[1] *De Anima*, Migne, CX, 1109.
[2] *De Universo*, Migne, CXI, 9–614.

to construct his book very much as Romans in the
Middle Ages plundered the Coliseum to build their
houses, Rabanus in turn takes most of his book from
Isidore, omitting the account of the liberal arts
he had written of elsewhere, expanding Isidore's
statements in places, borrowing also from Bede
in his chapter on chronology, from Lactantius for
the account of the Sibyls, and from Jerome for the
geography of Palestine and the explanation of
Hebrew names. But, instead of elaborating his
work in twenty books, as did Isidore, Rabanus had
enough matter for twenty-two. Now, although
twenty-two was not a sacred number, he was still
fortunate enough to chance on the fact that Jerome
had divided the whole of the Old Testament into
twenty-two books, thus furnishing him with a venerable, if not a sacred precedent. It is a dreary
enough task to read continuously such a work, but,
without some understanding of both the scope and
diversity of its contents, it is difficult to appreciate
what was the sum of knowledge of that time, or
the attitude of mind which an educator had to
encounter. An exhibition of its contents is a
decided help towards appreciating the confused
medley of general information, at best taken at
second or third hand, which was then accepted un-
questioningly as the body of settled truth. It is
also a help in the same way towards appreciating
the untrained and credulous condition of mind
which characterized not alone the uneducated but
even the clergy. Against such a background of

general misinformation how brightly does even the
slightest light shine! and how real is the contrast
between Rabanus, foolish as much of his writing
was, and the age he was attempting to educate!

But let us examine his encyclopedia. The
twenty-two books fall into two parts, the first five
dealing with sacred and the other seventeen with
secular knowledge. In spite of the apparent confusion, there is a thread of logical continuity which
holds the work together. Thus the order of subjects in the first five books is as follows: God,
then his creatures, celestial and terrestrial; that is
to say, angels and men. The account of the men
is confined to the Bible. Accordingly, first comes
Adam, with the other antediluvians following,
then the patriarchs with other notable Old Testament men and women, and then the prophets,
followed by New Testament persons and the mar-
tyrs. Next comes an account of the Church, with
chapters on the Church and the synagogue, religion
and faith, the clergy, the monks, and other orders
of the faithful, heresy and schism, definitions
relating to the true faith and church doctrine, and
account of the Scriptures, embracing some notice
of the authorship of each book, with a summary of
the contents. Then, by an odd but not unnatural
digression, we have a chapter on libraries, and
"The Diversity of Literary Works." This "diversity" relates to kinds of treatises that may be
written, the various parts of a discourse, the division into chapters and verses, and the material

make-up of books. Then follows a chapter on
the "canons of the Gospels," being a list of ten
patristic harmonies of the Gospels, followed by
other chapters on the decrees of the church coun-
cils, the Easter cycle, the canonical divisions of
the day and the appropriate duties attached
thereto, with closing chapters on sacrifices, sacraments, exorcisms, creeds, prayer and fasting, confession and penance. With this account of God,
his creatures, his Church, and the Scriptures, the
first five books close, the exposition of secular
knowledge beginning with the sixth book.

The sixth book is on "Man and his Parts," that
is to say, on human nature, and the various "parts"
or functions of the soul and body, explained literally, mystically and allegorically, all with proper
Scripture proof-texts. It includes also an explanation of the various postures and movements of the
body. Standing is thus symbolical of belief, for
the Apostle says, "Stand fast in the faith." The
closing chapter of the book is devoted to the parts
of the human body which in Scripture are said to
be parts of the devil's body. Among them are the
eyes, nostrils, tongue, mouth, bones, and even a
tail, inasmuch as "he swingeth his tail like a
cedar."

The seventh book is a sort of sequel to the sixth,
dealing with the periods of human life, the various
degrees of relationship by marriage, with two
chapters on monstrosities, such as the fauns, the
satyrs, the giants, the dog-headed men, Cerberus

and the Chimaera, and on "herds and beasts of burden," that is, the domestic animals.

The eighth book is zoölogical. It first gives an account of wild beasts in general, starting out with lions, panthers, pards, leopards, tigers, wolves, foxes, dogs, apes, "and all other animals that prey either with teeth or claws, excepting serpents." Every beast in the list has its natural description, and a special mystical meaning as well. The spotted pard, to take one example from many, is rich in significance. It "mystically signifies the devil, who is full of manifold wickedness." Again it typifies "the sinner covered with the spots of sin and of divers errors. Hence the prophet says, 'The pard cannot change his spots.'" It is also connected with the millennium, "when 'the pard shall lie down with the kid.'" And it stands for Antichrist, the beast in the Apocalypse, "which ascended from the sea, like unto a pard." After the wild beasts the "minute animals" are described. Such are crickets, frogs, ants, mice, moles and hedgehogs. The mole, condemned to perpetual blindness and darkness, is an emblem of idolatry. Among the ants enumerated is a kind said to be in Ethiopia, in shape like a dog. This dog-ant "digs up golden sands with its feet and keeps guard over them, lest any one steal the sand." Frogs are briefly described, and then spiritually stigmatized as "demons" and "heretics which cease not their vain and garrulous croaking." Separate chapters follow on serpents, worms, fishes

and birds. Then comes a description of the "minute birds." Some of these "birds" are flies.
Others are bees, wasps, locusts and ants, each of
them having a mystical significance. The bee signifies wisdom, and the locust has various meanings.
The fly and the mouse are said to have come originally from Greece. Flies, moreover, "after they
have been killed in water, will revive within the
space of an hour."

The ninth book is devoted to the world in general, its elements, the various planets, stars, and
constellations, and the phenomena of the atmos-
phere. Atoms are fully defined, and the four elements out of which everything has been made.
Then follows a general description of the heavens
and the two "doors" of heaven, namely, the east,
the west, because the sun enters by one and leaves
by the other. Then there are the two *cardines*, or
"turning-points," north and south. After a chapter
on light and another on celestial luminaries in general, there is a description of the sun, moon, stars,
and some of the constellations, with one on the
morning and another on the evening star. The rest
of the book deals with the air, clouds, thunder and
lightning, and other "coruscations," the rainbow,
fire, frost, coals, ashes, wind, breezes and calm
weather, whirlwinds and tempests. The book as
a whole is thus astronomical in its first part and in
the last part is meteorological. The tenth book is
on chronology, or "divisions of time." The eleventh
book, entitled "On the Diversity of Waters," is

aquatic throughout. Waters are classified in part as salt, fresh, bituminous and sulphurous, and the curative or magical virtues of the many springs and streams are expatiated upon. Then comes a description of various bodies of water, such as the ocean, the Mediterranean Sea, the Red Sea, the "abyss," bays and straits, lakes and pools, torrents and whirlpools, with chapters on rain and the two kinds of raindrops (*stilla*, the falling drop, and *gutta*, the fallen drop); the book closing with explanations of snow, ice, frost, hail, dew, mist and deluges. The twelfth and thirteenth books are occupied with a general geography of the earth. There is a chapter on paradise, and another on the "regions of the earth," which contains detailed topographical, historical and other descriptive mention of the various tribes and countries of the earth. Rabanus then proceeds to define and describe islands, promontories, mountains, hills, valleys, plains and forests. He closes the book with an account of "various places" of geographical character. First come "scriptural places," then "stormy places," followed by the "lairs of wild beasts," and then groves and deserts. After these come "devious places," "pleasant places," "sunny places," "warm places," "ship-building places," and lastly "slippery places." Last of all comes his account of shores, caves, chasms, "depths," "the pit," the site of Erebus and of the River Cocytus in the under world.

The fourteenth book is on "public buildings,"

but includes private dwellings under it. It is a manual of domestic and public architecture of the ancients, with full spiritual interpretation. The fifteenth book is on the philosophy, poetry and mythology of the ancients. The sixteenth book may be described as a sort of ethnology or sociology, as it contains an account of various nations of men, their languages, their forms of government, with definitions of civil and military terms. The seventeenth book is on "the dust and soil of the earth," that is to say, on minerals and metals. There is first the "soil found in waters," as salt and pitch. The "common stones" are next described. Such are "rock," "cliffs," flint, gypsum, sand and lime. Then come the "distinguished stones," such as jet, asbestus and selenite, the Persian moonstone, whose brightness "is said to wax and wane with the moon." Higher yet come the marbles and ivory, which are assigned separate chapters. After them there is a chapter on precious stones, followed by others on pearls, crystals and glass. The seven metals — gold, silver, brass, electrum, tin, lead and iron — conclude the book.

The eighteenth book deals with weights, measures, numbers, and musical and medical terms. The nineteenth is agricultural and botanical, describing in succession the various grains, leguminous plants, vines, trees, aromatic herbs and the common vegetables. The twentieth describes wars, and the different kinds of armor, the various athletic games, ship-building and blacksmithing.

The twenty-first deals with the domestic arts of
house-building, carpentering, weaving and spin-
ning, and explains fully the costumes of various
nations and the kinds of garments worn by men
and women.   The twenty-second details the various
household utensils and tools, beginning with tables,
eating and drinking vessels, going on to kitchen
utensils, baskets, lamps, couches and chairs, and
ending with garden tools and harness.

What a mass and a mess it all is!   It falls behind
the etymologies of Isidore in point of arrangement
and divisions of the material.   It is, moreover,
somewhat weakened and diluted.   Yet it is not
without a general plan.   He has, moreover, added
to Isidore's work much concrete information that
was useful for his time — no doubt more useful
then than Isidore's would have been.   Taken with
the other educational writings of Rabanus, it gives
a completeness to his activity as an educational
author which is proof of his sagacity; for he not
only furnished the men of his time with methods
and subjects on the formal side of education, but
met their empty ignorance with a vast collection
of the most useful common information that was
accessible to him, and so became the teacher of his
time both in regard to the substance of its secular
knowledge as well as on the side of method, thus
extending his labors far beyond the limits within
which Alcuin had worked.

CHAPTER VIII

ALCUIN'S LATER INFLUENCE

WHAT Alcuin had been to the whole of Frankland Rabanus was specifically to Germany, and, though his influence is discernible separately from the influence of his master, the two soon blended and carried forward for generations the educational tradition of Western Europe. The strength of the movement was at times centred in one or a few places and at others dispersed in many. As the main stream of learning had flowed from York to Tours and from Tours to Fulda, so it is again visible later as it passes from Fulda to Auxerre, touching Ferrieres, old and new Corbie, Reichenau, St. Gall, and Rheims, one branch of it finally reaching Paris. And yet the stream did not run unbroken, but with parallel lesser currents and connecting cross-streams, so that its general widening progress is as diversified as the fan-like sweep of a gulf-stream in the ocean, and can only be rightly measured by taking into account its entire extent. If the current was sometimes parted, it was not because the stream did not flow from one source, and if some places were touched only momentarily or left untouched altogether, it was because its volume was not vast enough to overspread the whole surface on which it flowed. And yet the influence of Alcuin is not easy to trace. There were no new institutions founded on the model of his teaching after his death, and, even in the institutions which had existed, the career of learning was irregular and fluctuating. Schools died out and were again revived in their old places, sometimes to continue for a time in power, sometimes to linger feebly or else to expire finally. Even the palace school of Charles entered on a career of fitful activity, changing first from Alcuin to Erigena, and then undergoing other mutations, never utterly extinct, and yet without leaving behind any continuous record of its doings. Therefore, instead of seeking to gather conclusions from the imperfect records of the fluctuating fortunes of certain places where schools were held, a surer way is to trace Alcuin's general influence through the succession of his immediate and remote pupils, for herein is to be seen the true inner continuity of education for a century and a half after his death, if not longer.

Before doing this, some mention of Erigena is in place. The Irish teaching which had crept into the palace school and caused Alcuin such unconcealed anxiety shortly before his death received a new and strong impetus after he was gone. In 814 Charles the Great died, and his son Lewis the Pious succeeded him. Soon after Lewis died the youthful king, Charles the Bald, made John Scotus Erigena master of the palace school about 845.

Lewis had been careful to keep within the limits laid down by Alcuin, but his successor was of a different temper, and welcomed the acute and witty representative of the dangerous speculative learning that was so well fitted to shake unquestioning faith in tradition. John brought with him the proscribed Martianus Capella, and extended the influence of this writer by composing a commentary. When appealed to by Hincmar of Rheims to come and help the orthodox faith with his pen, he did not hesitate to quote Greek as well as Latin fathers, and even heathen philosophers whenever convenient, as authorities fit to be cited side by side with Scripture; while, as Mr. Mullinger aptly observes, "to fill up the measure of his offence, he referred with undisguised approval to the pages of Martianus Capella."[1] The contest had set in between speculation and tradition, and could no longer be confined within the bounds Alcuin would have approved, and the new influence issuing from the teaching of Erigena, though at first resisted, afterwards gradually mingled with the old instruction given in the monasteries.

But let us return to the more prominent of the later pupils who represent the influence of Alcuin, many of them through Rabanus.

Servatus Lupus (805–862) was educated in the monastery of Ferrieres under Aldrich, the pupil of Alcuin. When Aldrich became archbishop of Sens, he despatched his pupil to Fulda, where he

[1] *Schools of Charles the Great,* p. 186.

studied under Rabanus, then at the height of his reputation. In 836, after a brilliant career as a student of letters, as well as in theology, he returned to Frankland. Aldrich died soon after, and Servatus Lupus succeeded him in 842 as abbat of Ferrieres, where he taught with distinction, gathering about him numerous disciples and a considerable library, becoming himself the one purely literary man of his time and cultivating the classical writers to an extent unheard of for centuries. While at Fulda he often repaired to Seligenstadt to consult Einhard, the biographer of Charles the Great, whose friendship he had made and who then ruled the abbey of Seligenstadt, where there were many books. Einhard's taste for letters and friendship for Servatus promoted his progress in study and thus supplemented the instruction of Fulda.

Haymo, a fellow-pupil with Rabanus at Fulda and one of his companions later under the instruction of Alcuin at Tours, returned from Tours to Fulda, where he taught in the school for some time. He left Fulda in 841, to become bishop of Halberstadt, and died in 853.

Walafrid Strabo (born 807), after pursuing his first studies as a boy at the school of Reichenau, on Lake Constance, was sent thence to Fulda to study under Rabanus. From Fulda he returned to Reichenau, and, after directing the school of that abbey for several years, was elected its abbat in 842. He transplanted thither the studies of Fulda, and to his repute as a teacher added considerable accomplishment as a poet. His fame was probably greater than his merit. His undisputed merit, however, consists in his extension of the teaching of his master. *"Docuit multos"* is the testimony of Rabanus himself, in the epitaph he composed for Walafrid, and indicates that his scholars were numerous enough to call for special mention.

Rudolph (800?–866), a monk of Fulda, was both the pupil and biographer of Rabanus, succeeding him in the care of the abbey school. Though of course far inferior to his master, he was thought a man of great learning, and continued the methods of Rabanus, though with less ability. Ermenric, one of his scholars, who afterwards became abbat of Ellwangen, testifies, in a work addressed to him, to the profundity of his erudition and his success as a teacher.

Liutpert, the capable abbat of New Corbie, who died in 853, had also been a monk at Fulda, with Rabanus as the master of his studies. He also served as the first abbat of Hirschau, a community of monks who had gone out from Fulda by the commission of Rabanus. The monk Maginhard was also at Fulda about the same time.

Paschasius Ratpert (died 865) retired from the world to the monastery of Corbie, then governed by Adelhard. He applied himself to study with such success as to be selected to instruct his fellow-pupils. Cicero and Terence were favorite writers with him before he had entered the monastery. His activity and diligence were marked. He accompanied Adelhard to found the abbey of New Corbie in Saxony. He taught many pupils, and among them the younger Adelhard, Anscharius, archbishop of Hamburg, Hildemann and Odo, each of whom became bishop of Beauvais, and Warin, later abbat of New Corbie. In 844, he was himself made abbat of old Corbie, where he died in 865. His pupil, Odo of Beauvais, succeeded him as abbat.

Among other monks of old Corbie who deserve mention was Ratramnus, whose knowledge of the arts was considerable and whose ecclesiastical reading embraced not only the Latin but the Greek fathers. He entered the monastery probably about the time Adelhard became its abbat, and died there, having passed all his life as a simple monk, without aspiring to any preferment. Among his friends were Servatus Lupus and Odo of Beauvais. Another monk of the monastery of New Corbie in Saxony, who may be connected with the influence of Alcuin and Rabanus, was Rembert, who was consecrated a monk by Anscharius, whom he succeeded as archbishop of Hamburg in 856.

Passing notice may be given to Hilduin, the fellow-pupil of Servatus Lupus and later abbat of St. Denis, who died in 840, and Ado (800?–875), archbishop of Vienne, who had been offered in youth to the monastery of Ferrieres by his parents, and was educated there under Servatus Lupus.

Werembert (died 884) pursued his youthful studies at Fulda under Rabanus Maurus, and then went

to the important abbey of St. Gall. One of his
fellow-students under Rabanus was Otfried of
Weissenburg. Werembert was proficient, according to the chroniclers of his time, both in Latin and
Greek, the fine arts, philosophy, poetry, music,
and sculpture, as well as theology and history.
We know little of his life beyond the fact that he
was a monk of St. Gall and taught for a long time.
Grimaldus, abbat of St. Gall, was educated in the
monastery of Reichenau, where his education was
touched by the influence of Alcuin and Rabanus
through his friend Ermenric, the monk of Reichenau, who had been a pupil of Walafrid Strabo.
Harmot (died 884), a friend and fellow-pupil with
Werembert, virtually governed the abbey of St.
Gall even during the lifetime of Grimaldus. When
Grimaldus died, Harmot was unanimously elected
to succeed him. He was a writer of various treatises and also enriched the abbey library greatly.

Three monks of St. Gall, closely connected by
reason of their warm personal friendship for each
other and their common distinction as scholars,
were Ratbert, Notker, and Tutilo, who, though
apparently not educated by teachers in the direct
line of succession from Alcuin and Rabanus, were
yet familiar with the writings of these masters.
Of the three, Notker may be singled out for separate
mention. He entered St. Gall as a pupil about
840, and after a while became head of the inner
school, the monastery then containing an inner
school for the *oblati,* who were offered for monastic

life, and an outer school for the *externi*. In one of his commentaries he ranks the writings of Rabanus with Jerome, Augustine and Chrysostom, and in another work extols the grammar of Alcuin as eclipsing even that of Priscian himself. Among those touched by Notker's influence were Regino, the abbat of Prum, and Robert, bishop of Metz.

Turning from St. Gall to Auxerre in Frankland, the influence of Alcuin and Rabanus again appears as a dominating impulse.

Eric of Auxerre (about 834–881), when a boy, entered the monastery of St. Germain at Auxerre. After pursuing his early studies at that place he went to Fulda, where he was instructed by Haymo, and afterwards to Ferrieres, where Servatus Lupus was his master. When the period of his study under Servatus was completed he returned to Auxerre, and was given charge of the monastery school of St. Germain in that place. Among his pupils were Hucbald and the famous Remy of Auxerre.

Hucbald (died about 930), the monk of St. Amand, was regarded as the leading teacher of his time next to Remy. He was a nephew of Milo, the Christian poet and student of both the liberal and fine arts, who had studied under a pupil of Alcuin. He pursued his earlier studies under the superintendence of his uncle, and then passed from St. Amand to the monastery of St. Germain at Auxerre, where he completed his course under Eric in company with Remy and other pupils of note.

His proficiency in the arts was notable to such an
extent that one of his eulogists asserts "he was so
distinguished for his skill in the liberal arts, that
he was compared with the ancient philosophers."

The most famous teacher in Frankland, as the
ninth century passed away and the tenth opened,
was Remy of Auxerre. He early became a monk
at the abbey of St. Germain, where his teacher
was Eric of Auxerre, the pupil of Haymo and
Servatus Lupus. Among his fellow-pupils was,
as has been said, the celebrated Hucbald, the monk
of Amand. On the death of Eric he succeeded to
the charge of the school. Soon after he was called
away in company with Hucbald by summons of
Fulco, archbishop of Rheims, to re-establish the
schools of that diocese which had fallen into decay.
Remy taught both the liberal arts and theology, and
among his auditors was the archbishop himself.
The scholars whom Remy taught and their successors continued the school at Rheims well through
the tenth century, and among the later pupils of
the school were the historian Frodoard, Abbo of
Fleury, and Hildebold and Blidulph, two pupils
of Remy himself who were influential in establishing schools in Lorraine. When Fulco died, Remy
went from Rheims to Paris, where he established a
public, not a monastic school, open to all and free
from ecclesiastical rule. Here he taught philosophy
and the liberal arts, as well as theology, expounding the treatise *On the Categories* then attributed
to Augustine, and teaching the liberal arts gener-

ally with Martianus Capella as the text-book, thus
finally establishing that hitherto suspected author
in a place of honor. To render Martianus more
easily understood, he wrote an elaborate commentary. Out of this school, "the first cradle
of the University of Paris," [1] came Odo, abbat of
Cluny, the greatest pupil of Remy. It is doubtless true that Remy marks a new period in the
revival of studies, and some have considered his
influence comparable to that of Alcuin or Rabanus.
Though this cannot be shown, it is yet fair to say,
in the words of an old chronicler, that "the studies
which had become obsolete for a long time began
to flourish again under him, and indeed sprang up,
as it were, newly born from his teaching." [2] Among
his writings were commentaries on the grammarians,
Donatus and Priscian, and a treatise on music, besides his already-mentioned exposition of Martianus
Capella.

Odo of Cluny (880–942) was offered by his parents
while yet a child to the monastery of St. Martin
at Tours, but did not at once become a monk.
After passing his youth in secular life, he returned
to Tours at the age of nineteen and became a canon
of St. Martin. His marked taste for Virgil and
the other ancient authors on the side of literature
was supplemented by the study of Priscian on the
side of grammar. He soon conceived a desire of
studying the arts with more thoroughness and went

---

[1] *Histoire Littéraire de la France*, VI, p. 100.
[2] *Histoire Littéraire de la France*, VI, p. 101.

from Tours to Paris, where Remy of Auxerre was giving public lectures. Under him Odo studied dialectics and music with special attention, and all the other liberal arts. On returning to Tours he is said, on uncertain authority, to have had charge of the abbey school. Soon after he resolved to renounce the world finally and give himself to monastic life. When in his thirtieth year he entered a monastery in Burgundy, taking with him "one hundred books," probably his whole library. After the death of the abbat in 927, Odo was elected to succeed him, and became not only the head of that monastery, but of the more important abbey of Cluny and others. He was influential in bringing about a general monastic reform in Frankland and in connection therewith the establishment of a large number of schools. One of these was the school at Fleury. Another was revived in the abbey of Gorz, near Metz, whither many pupils of the school at Rheims went to form a learned monastic community. He also established instruction at the abbey of St. Julian of Tours, where he himself spent some time. His reputation spread rapidly, and he was consulted by the pope and by princes, as Rabanus had been before. He made three journeys to Rome. His death occurred about 942.

Such were the men who continued the influence of Alcuin and Rabanus down to the middle of the tenth century. They and their associates sat in the high places of education under the successors of Charles the Great. But they were not all, for

history fails to preserve a record of their times
with completeness. It is, therefore, only fair to
presume that they embody less than the full influence of the movement started by Alcuin, though
undoubtedly the greatest part of it. In this succession the names that stand out pre-eminent are
those of Servatus Lupus, Walafrid Strabo, Paschasius Ratpert, Werembert, Eric of Auxerre,
Hucbald, Remy of Auxerre and Odo of Cluny.

The middle of the tenth century marks the
limit of what may be styled the age of Alcuin
in education, for at this point his direct influence gradually disappears, and yet, amid the dev-
astations and wars of the age that followed, there
are indications of the continuance of schools trace-
able to the influences of the preceding age. The
pupils of Odo of Cluny were numerous, and the
school of Rheims, revived by Remy and Hucbald,
had the great Gerbert, afterwards Pope Sylvester
the Second, for a time as its master. The many
pupils of Odo and Gerbert maintained almost un-
aided the cause of education at the end of the
tenth century. At this point the passing-on of
learning from hand to hand becomes too obscure
to follow, but early in the eleventh century schools
are again discernible in the principal monasteries,
taught by masters who could have received the
tradition of learning only from the men of the last
century. Meanwhile Paris was assuming more and
more the character of a metropolis, having become
the fixed residence of royalty. The schools near

by, including Tours, Bec in Normandy, and Chartres, became more closely connected with the capital, and with the increase of intellectual speculation and controversy there came a great increase of masters and pupils. The time was ripe for repeating the prophetic experiment of Remy. A new succession of teachers arose. One of them was Drogo, who had as a pupil John the Deaf. John the Deaf, in turn, instructed Roscellinus of Chartres, and about Roscellinus clusters that brilliant galaxy of disciples, Peter of Cluny, Odo of Cambray, William of Champeaux, and Abelard.[1] We are now at the opening of the twelfth century. Old things have passed away and with the opening of the University of Paris the new age of scholasticism has fully set in.

Eulogists of Alcuin have sought to do him the surpassing honor of adjudging him the true ancestor of the University of Paris and thereby of the universities of modern Europe. The claim scarcely needs to be more than mentioned before it is refuted. Neither on the side of instruction nor of external organization did he entertain conceptions which would naturally have produced such a result, nor is there any evidence that, without the intellectual awakening that came to Europe under the name of scholasticism, the universities would have been founded, or, if founded, that they would have been capable of the development to which they attained. The awakening impulse came from with-

[1] Monnier, *Alcuin et Charlemagne*, pp. 266-268.

out, through the introduction of the philosophical
works of Greek genius in Latin versions made
from the intermediary Arabic. It was these that
quickened the almost lifeless learning and education of Europe. But, admitting this without
reserve, it yet remains true that the schools of
the cathedrals and monasteries, the natural successors and heirs of Alcuin, were the centres of
student life and of the teaching tradition. Without the existence of such centres, established as
they had been for generations, it is doubtful
whether universities would have arisen.

Alcuin's work was incipient and premonitory,
and the outcome was greater than his plan. But
his work had first to be done before later develop-
ments were possible. It had a distinctive life of
its own, which seems to have been spent by the end
of the tenth century. But there are no absolute
breaks in human history. Therefore, when from
the middle of the tenth century to the middle of
the eleventh the teachers and schools that descend
from him are nearly or wholly lost to view, let it
not be assumed that their influence ceased. It was
a time of great confusion and of consequent loss of
historic records. The little learning that lingered,
however, is not to be despised, though it glim-
mered feebly enough in the darkness, for it was
the only learning. When, therefore, new and
unrevolutionary teachers appear later, whom it is
not possible to connect by express evidence with
the men of the century before, it is to be presumed

that they took up and carried forward an existing tradition, which, though obscure to us, was plain to them. There was but one tradition available for their use, and that flowed from the schools of the age quickened by Alcuin.

APPENDIX

EDITIONS OF ALCUIN

I. FROBEN'S EDITION IN VOLUMES C AND CI
OF MIGNE'S *Patrologia Latina.*

THE first edition of Alcuin's collected works was
edited by Duchesne and printed at Paris in 1617.
Various scattered treatises, not included in this
edition, were afterwards discovered and printed.
In 1777 Froben, the prince-abbat of St. Emmeran at
Ratisbon, brought out a far more complete edition
than had yet appeared, with an improved text and
a vast amount of illustrative and critical matter.
This edition of Froben, with the addition of Alcuin's commentary on the Apocalypse, which was
brought to light in 1837, is reprinted in volumes
C and CI of Migne's *Patrologia Latina*, published
at Paris in 1863. Migne's reprint contains the
most complete collection of Alcuin's works, including all the chief treatises known to have been
written by him. It is doubtful if any of his writings remain in manuscript to be added to the list
of works printed in Migne, beyond a few minor
treatises and a very considerable number of letters,
some of which have been since edited by Jaffé and

Duemmler.   The arrangement of Alcuin's writings
in Migne is as follows : —

I. Epistles, Vol. C, 135–515.

Of the two hundred and thirty-two letters, two
are written by Charles (Nos. lxxxi and clviii)
and the rest are by Alcuin. Fully five-sixths of
them are written between 796, when he went to
Tours, and 804, — the last eight years of his life.
They may accordingly be taken as containing his
final opinions in regard to whatever matters they
treat.   His best literary style is also in them, the
Latinity having as a rule both more fluency and
propriety than in his other writings.[1] Some of
them are long and carefully composed in set form,
containing many of his favorite epistolary flourishes or *deflorationes*, while others are in the light-
est vein. The subject-matter is by turns theological,
moral, ecclesiastical, political, didactic, and personal and well reflects his varied activities.   His
chief correspondents were Charles the Great and
Arno.   We have over thirty of his letters to each

[1] Alcuin's style in general is far removed from pure Latinity.
It is inferior to that of Einhard, the biographer of Charles, who
had fair success in writing after as good a model as Suetonius,
whereas nothing of Alcuin's approaches this. His faults, or
rather the apparently ineradicable faults of his time, touch the
elementary questions of syntax. For example, he uses the tenses
incorrectly in subordinate sequences, joins *ut* in final clauses
indifferently with the indicative or subjunctive, writes a participle where a finite verb is in place, and often employs the plu-
perfect where he ought to use the perfect. Compare *Monumenta
Alcuiniana*, pp. 36 and 38.

of them. His other correspondents include the Pope, the patriarchs of Jerusalem and of Aquileia, kings in Britain, members of the imperial family in Frankland, archbishops, bishops, monasteries, and his pupils. Of all his writings, the letters have the highest historical value, being of capital importance for understanding the chief questions in Church and State during the latter half of the eighth century.

II. Exegetical Works, 515–1155.

1. *Questions and Answers on Genesis,* 515–569.

This is dedicated to his pupil Sigulf. It is partly indebted to Jerome's *Quæstiones in Genesin* and to St. Gregory's *Moralia.*

2. *Enchiridion, or Brief Exposition of Certain Psalms,* 569–639.

These are the seven penitential Psalms, the 118th (our 119th) Psalm, and the fifteen "gradual" Psalms. It is apparently an original composition, and was dedicated to Arno, who had asked Alcuin to compose such a treatise.

3. *Commentary on the Song of Solomon,* 639–655.

Probably an original composition. It is dedicated to no one by name, though in the prefixed verses a certain *juvenis,* probably a pupil, is exhorted to read it. At the end of it is added the *Epistola ad Daphnin,* a short commentary on the text in Solomon's Song, "There are threescore queens and fourscore concubines."

4. *Commentary on Ecclesiastes*, 665–723.

In the preface to this commentary, Alcuin says, "I have composed a short commentary on this book out of the works of the holy fathers and partly from the commentary of Jerome." It is dedicated to his pupils, Onias, Candidus, and Nathanael.

5. *Interpretations of the Hebrew Names of our Lord's Progenitors*, 723–733.

It is dedicated to Charles and is based on Bede's *Homily on the Nativity of the Blessed Virgin Mary*.

6. *Commentary on the Gospel of St. John*, 733–1007.

Alcuin's principal exegetical work, written about 800 and dedicated to Gisela, the sister, and Rotrud, the daughter, of Charles. It is based principally upon Augustine, Ambrose, Gregory and Bede.

7. *A Treatise on St. Paul's Epistles to Titus, Philemon, and to the Hebrews*, 1007–1083.

There is no dedication. The comments on Titus and Philemon are compiled from Jerome's commentaries on those epistles. The comments on Hebrews are also compiled from the Latin version of Chrysostom's commentary on Hebrews made by Mutianus.

8. *A Brief Commentary on Some Sayings of St. Paul*, 1083–1086.

This short note may be original in part, though but only in part, for Jerome on Hebrews can be traced in it.

9. *Commentary on the Apocalypse*, 1086–1156.

Part of the treatise appears to be lost, as the

exposition breaks off abruptly in chapter xii.
Possibly, however, Alcuin did not complete the
work. It is based on Bede's *Commentary on
the Apocalypse*, with supplementary use of the
writings of Augustine, Jerome, Victorinus, Tycho-
nius, Primasius, and Ambrose Autpert, one of
Alcuin's contemporaries.

III. DOGMATIC WORKS, Vol. CI, 9–303.

1. *On the Trinity*, 9–63.

Written in Tours toward the close of Alcuin's life
and dedicated to Charles after he had become emperor. Augustine's treatise *On the Holy Trinity*
is Alcuin's chief reliance. Alcuin's *Twenty-Eight
Questions on the Trinity*, dedicated to his pupil
Fridugis, are appended.

2. *On the Procession of the Holy Spirit*, 63–83.

A collection of testimonies from Scripture and
the fathers, dedicated to Charles.

3. *Writings against Felix of Urgel and Elipandus
of Toledo*, 83–303.

These contain an elaborate argument, based on
the fathers, exhibiting the Catholic faith as against
the Adoptionist heresy. They show much vigor
and contain Alcuin's ablest work.

IV. LITURGICAL AND MORAL WORKS, 439–655.

1. *Book of Sacraments*, 445–465.
2. *On the Psalms*, 465–509.
3. *Offices for the Dead*, 509–611.
4. *On the Ceremonies of Baptism*, 611–613.

These four contain the forms of worship, both general and special, for ecclesiastical service. They are excerpted and arranged from older liturgies.

5. *On the Virtues and Vices,* 613–639.

A moral treatise dedicated to Count Wido and taken from Augustine.

6. *On the Nature of the Soul,* 639–649.

This is also taken from Augustine, and is dedicated to Gundrada (Eulalia).

7. *On the Confession of Sins,* 649–655.

A short letter of exhortation addressed to the monks of St. Martin at Tours.

V. LIVES OF THE SAINTS, 655–723.

1. *The Life of St. Martin of Tours,* 657–663.
2. *The Life of St. Vedast,* 663–681.
3. *Life of St. Riquier,* 681–690.
4. *Life of St. Willibrord,* 690–723.

VI. POEMS, 723–847.

1. *Miscellaneous Poems,* 723–812.

These include prayers, inscriptions for books, metrical histories of the Old and New Testaments, inscriptions for churches and altars, hortatory moral verses, miscellaneous inscriptions, poems to different friends, epitaphs, epigrams, and riddles. The metres employed are almost exclusively the dactylic hexameter or the elegiac. They are not conformed to a strict regard for quantity, but are probably better than most of the poetry of that time in this respect. As poetry, they have little claim to admiration, though there are not wanting many touches of description and imagination that are pleasant.

2. *Poem on the Saints of the Church at York,* 812–847.

This poem in heroic verse is Alcuin's history of the Church at York, partly based on Bede's writings and partly on his own personal knowledge. It appears to have been composed shortly before he went to Frankland. It consists of 1657 hexameter verses, modeled to a considerable extent on Virgil and attempting a sustained dignity of style. Its value for the history of Alcuin's connection with York is, of course, very great.

VII. DIDACTIC WORKS, 847–1001.

(For an analysis of these didactic writings see the fifth chapter of this volume.)

1. *Grammar,* 847–901.

2. *Orthography,* 901–919.

3. *Dialogue on Rhetoric and the Virtues,* 919–949.

4. *Dialectics,* 949–975.

5. *Disputation of the Royal and Most Noble Youth Pippin with Albinus the Scholastic,* 975–979.

6. *On the Calculation of Easter,* 979–1001.

VIII. WORKS DOUBTFULLY ASCRIBED TO ALCUIN, 1001–1169.

Two of these are of interest :

1. *The Disputation of the Boys,* 1097–1143, and

2. *The Propositions of Alcuin for Whetting the Wit of Youth,* 1143–1161.

IX. SPURIOUS WORKS, 1173–1297.

II. *Monumenta Alcuiniana a Philippo Jafféo Præparata. Ediderunt Wattenbach et Duemmler.* pp. vi + 912. Berlin, 1873.

This is the sixth volume in the *Bibliotheca Rerum Germanicarum* begun under the editorial care of Jaffé, who died in 1870. Wattenbach and Duemmler carried on the work interrupted by Jaffé's untimely death. The volume they have edited contains the following documents : —

1. *The Life of Alcuin,* composed in the year 829 by an anonymous biographer, who states that he was a pupil of Sigulf. It is of distinct value.

To this the following writings of Alcuin are subjoined : —

2. *Life of St. Willibrord.*

3. *Poem on the Saints of the Church at York.*

4. *Epistles.*

The Epistles are edited by Duemmler, and the other three documents by Wattenbach. Their editing is a model in every way. If only the rest of Alcuin could be as faithfully revised, the service rendered to learning would indeed be great.

The text is thoroughly purged after a scientific method, variant readings are indicated so far as significant, and the body of interpretative matter and cross-references, printed at the foot of each page, gives abundant illustration of the bearings of the text. The Epistles, which are of such prime intrinsic importance, fill the chief part of the book.

Their number is largely increased, so that we may now consult two hundred and ninety-two of Alcuin's composition, besides fourteen letters written by others and connected with his correspondence. Their chronology is cleared up and other obscurities are fully explained for the first time. The poem *On the Saints of the Church at York* is also elucidated by useful notes, and particularly by the references to Bede's *Ecclesiastical History* printed on the margin.

TABLE OF DATES

I

B.C. 384–322 Aristotle. His writings mark the highest development of Greek doctrine respecting education.

100–46 Cicero. Frequent notices of the arts of the Greeks, which by his time had become the groundwork of Roman culture.

116–27 Varro. His *Libri Novem Disciplinarum*, the thesaurus of information on the arts for later Latin writers.

8–A.D. 65 Seneca. *Epistle to Lucilius* on liberal studies and other references to education. He draws from Varro.

A.D. 35–96 Quintilian. *Institutio Oratoria*, partly on education. Varro his authority.

II

354–430 Augustine. Wrote *Disciplinarum Libri* shortly after his conversion. Other writings with educational bearings are *De Doctrina Christiana*, *De Ordine*, and *Retractiones*. Varro is his great authority.

Before 439 Martianus Capella's book *De Nuptiis Philologiæ et Mercuriæ*.

481–525 Boethius. Various translations and commentaries.

468–569 Cassidorus. *De Artibus ac Disciplinis Liberalium Litterarum*

—— –636 Isidore. Compiled the *Etymologiæ*, the first encyclopedia.

193

III

About 650 Christian Irish learning passing into Britain.

669 Theodore of Tarsus comes to Canterbury.

628–690 Benedict Biscop founds Wearmouth and Yarrow, where was represented all the learning of the West.

673–735 Bede, the pupil of Benedict Biscop.

732 Egbert, the friend of Bede, becomes archbishop of York and founds the cathedral school there.

IV

About 735 Alcuin born in Northumbria at or near York.

742 Charles the Great born, — son of Pepin, king of the Franks, and grandson of Charles Martel.

Before 745 Alcuin enters the school at York, founded by archbishop Egbert and conducted by Ælbert.

766 Egbert dies; Ælbert succeeds him as archbishop; Alcuin becomes master of the school at York. Alcuin, in company with Ælbert, visits Frankland and perhaps Rome also.

771 Charles becomes sole king of the Franks.

776 Rabanus Maurus born at Mayence.

780 Alcuin visits Italy, meeting Charles at Pavia. Ælbert dies.

781 Alcuin again visits Italy to obtain from the Pope the pallium for his fellow-pupil, the elder Eanbald, who had succeeded Ælbert as archbishop of York. At Parma he meets Charles, who invites him to come and teach at his court.

782 Alcuin leaves York to become master of the palace school at Aachen.

787 Charles, returning home from a visit to Italy,

brings into Frankland masters of grammar
and arithmetic. In the same year he issues
his great Capitulary promoting education.
This is followed by other injunctions to the
same effect in 788, 789, and as late as 802.

790–792 Alcuin revisits Britain.

792 Alcuin returns to Aachen to combat the disturb-
ing heresies of Adoptionism and image-worship.

794 Alcuin participates in the proceedings of the
Council at Frankfort, which condemns Adoptionism and image-worship.

796 Alcuin appointed abbat of Tours.

800 In June Charles visits Alcuin at Tours, accompanied by Queen Liutgard, who dies there.
Alcuin goes with Charles to Aachen, where
he engages in public debate with Felix of
Urgel, who acknowledges himself overcome
and retracts his Adoptionist errors.

800 On Christmas day in Rome Charles is crowned
Emperor of the Holy Roman Empire by the
Pope.

802 Rabanus Maurus studies under Alcuin at Tours.

804 On May 19th Alcuin dies and is buried at Tours.
The chief posts of educational advantage are
in possession of his friends or pupils.

Theodulf is virtual minister of education to
Charles the Great, Arno archbishop of Salz-
burg, Riculf of Mayence, Rigbod of Treves,
Leidrad of Lyons and Eanbald II of York.
Fridugis succeeds Alcuin as abbat of St. Mar-
tin at Tours, Augilbert is abbat of St. Riquier,
Sigulf of Ferrieres, Adelhard of Corbie near
Amiens, St. Benedict of Aniane in Languedoc,
and Rabanus is in charge of the school at
Fulda.

V

814 On June 28th Charles the Great dies and is buried at Aachen. Lewis the Pious succeeds him.

821 Aldrich, a pupil of Alcuin at Tours, succeeds Sigulf as abbat of Ferrieres.

822 Rabanus becomes abbat of Fulda. Adelhard founds the monastery of New Corbie in Saxony, becoming its first abbat, and continuing as abbat of old Corbie also.

842 Servatus Lupus, educated under Aldrich at Ferrieres and Rabanus at Fulda, succeeds Aldrich as abbat of Ferrieres.

Walafrid Strabo, pupil of Rabanus, becomes abbat of Reichenau.

Rabanus retires from the rule of Fulda.

845 John Scotus Erigena master of the palace school.

856 Rabanus dies near Mayence.

865 Paschasius Ratpert, pupil of Adelhard and abbat of old Corbie, dies.

By 870–880 The influence of Alcuin and Rabanus reaches St. Gall, being represented there by Werembert, Grimaldus, Notker and others.

881 Death of Eric of Auxerre. He was educated at Fulda under Haymo, the pupil of Alcuin and fellow-student with Rabanus, and at Ferrieres under Servatus Lupus, the pupil of Aldrich.

About 900 Remy of Auxerre, educated in company with Hucbald under Eric of Auxerre, opens his public school in Paris.

942 Death of Odo of Cluny, who had been educated at Tours and later under Remy at Paris.

About 950–1000 Education sustained almost entirely by pupils of Odo and Gerbert, for a while master of the school at Rheims revived by Remy and Hucbald.

BOOKS ON ALCUIN

The following list contains a selection of books and articles of interest on Alcuin. Those marked with an asterisk are especially helpful.

Adamson: *Alcuin*, in Leslie Stephen's *Dictionary of National Biography*.

Bahrdt: *Alcuin der Lehrer Karls des Grossen*. Lauenburg, 1861.

* Ceillier: *Histoire Générale des Auteurs Sacrés et Ecclésiastiques*, Vol. XII. Paris, 1862.

Corbet: *Hagiographie du Diocèse d'Amiens*, Vol. I. Paris and Amiens, 1868.

* Duemmler: *Alcuin*, in the *Allgemeine Deutsche Biographie*.

Dupuy: *Alcuin et l'École de St. Martin de Tours*. Tours, 1876.

Hamelin: *Essai sur la Vie et les Ouvrages d'Alcuin*. Rennes, 1873.

* *Histoire Litéraire de la France*, Vols. IV, V, VI. Paris, 1866.

Laforêt: *Alcuin Restaurateur des Sciences en Occident sous Charlemagne*. Louvain, 1851.

Lorenz: *Alcuins Leben*. Halle, 1829.

* Lorenz: *The Life of Alcuin*, translated from the German by Jane Mary Slee. London, 1837.

Meier: *Ausgewählte Schriften von Columban, Alcuin, u.s.w.*, in Vol. III of the *Bibliothek der katholischen Pädagogik*. Freiburg im Breisgau, 1890.

* Monnier: *Alcuin et Charlemagne*. Paris, 1864.

197

Monnier: *Alcuin et son influence littéraire, religieuse, et politique sur les Franks.*   Paris, 1853.

* Mullinger: *The Schools of Charles the Great.*   London, 1877.

Sickel: *Alcuinstudien,* in the *Journal of the Vienna Academy of Science,* Vol. LXXIX, pp. 461–550.   Vienna, 1875.

* Stubbs: *Alcuin,* in the *Dictionary of Christian Biography.*

Thery: *Alcuin (L'École et l'Académie Palatines).*   Amiens, 1878.

* Werner: *Alcuin und sein Jahrhundert.*   Vienna, 1881.

Rabanus Maurus: *Collected Works* in *Migne's Patrologia Latina,* Vols. CVII–CXII.

INDEX

199